Mastering Ceramic Glazing Techniques for Stunning Results

Mercy .S Hull

Mastering Ceramic Glazing Techniques for Stunning Results : Unlock the Secrets to Perfecting Ceramic Glazing for Jaw-Dropping Artwork

Funny helpful tips:

Stay positive; a positive mindset can enhance overall health and resilience.

Invest in employee well-being; a motivated team boosts productivity.

Life advices:

Rotate reading based on goals; whether for career, personal growth, or leisure, align your reading accordingly.

Incorporate interval training; it boosts metabolism and can lead to more effective fat burning.

Introduction

This beginner's guide to ceramic glazing and firing techniques covers a wide range of topics. It begins by exploring the history of ceramics and glazes, providing a historical context for this art form. The guide then delves into the science behind glazes, explaining temperature classifications, glaze composition, and their essential properties.

Readers are introduced to various methods of applying glaze, such as brushing, dipping, pouring, and spraying. The guide not only explains these techniques but also discusses their advantages and disadvantages, allowing beginners to make informed choices.

Safety and equipment play a crucial role in ceramic work, and the guide addresses these aspects comprehensively. It covers the necessary safety gear, tools for glaze preparation, work surfaces, and kiln equipment. This ensures that beginners are well-prepared and protected throughout the ceramic creation process.

Different types of glazes are explored, including considerations like firing temperature, kiln type, and intended use. This knowledge empowers beginners to choose the right glazes for their projects.

The guide also provides practical recipes for creating custom ceramic glazes, emphasizing the benefits of customization. It explains the components of glazes, how to develop recipes, and where to obtain glaze ingredients. This section equips beginners with the skills to mix their own glazes.

Lastly, the guide touches on kiln usage and offers valuable tips for beginners to ensure safe and effective firing of their ceramic pieces. It concludes by discussing potential career paths for ceramic artists, encouraging them to explore opportunities within the ceramics community. Overall, this guide serves as a comprehensive resource for those starting their journey in ceramic artistry.

Contents

Chapter One: History of Ceramics and Glazes

It's important to understand the history of ceramics in general and glazes specifically in order to fully appreciate the artistry of this work. The production of ceramics has a long history, dating back thousands of years. It was probably an accidental discovery that clay, something found in abundance, could be so easily formed into various types of objects when mixed with water. Once humans discovered that, however, it changed everything. Let's begin by discussing the history of ceramics.

History of Ceramics

The most ancient ceramic artifact known to date is a statuette of a woman that dates to 28,000 years BCE (before the common era-- it's synonymous with BC). This figurine is called the Venus of Dolní Věstonice (see the image above), and it was found in what is now the Czech Republic near Brno. The time period to which this dates is called the late Paleolithic period. Paleolithic just means Old Stone Age.

At this same location, there were hundreds of clay figurines of various animals uncovered close to the remains of a kiln shaped like a horseshoe. The Venus figurine is of a woman who appears to be pregnant. Many experts feel the so-called Venus figurines of women may have been representations of goddesses as women may have been perceived as the givers of life.

Ceramics first appear in Eastern Asia around 18,000 to 17,000 BCE in the Xianrendong Cave in China. Archaeologists believe that the use of pottery spread from China to Japan and the far eastern regions of Russia. There, ceramic shards dating to 14,000 BCE have been found.

Around 10,000 BCE, human populations were pressured by climate change to make alterations to the way they lived if they wanted to remain in sedentary communities. Those communities that began to manipulate plants to control their growth were successfully able to stay in sedentary enclaves rather than return to a hunting and gathering way of life. This was the birth of the domestication of plants and animals, and it is called the Neolithic period, or New Stone Age.

During the Neolithic time period, the use of ceramics was much more utilitarian, and therefore, increased significantly. As people established settled communities that practiced agriculture, clay-based ceramics became popular containers to hold food and water as well as other tools and materials. Archaeologists have documented their use as containers as early as 9,000 BCE, and they spread throughout Asia, the Middle East, and Europe.

These early ceramics were either just sun-dried or fired at low temperatures--below about 1,800 degrees Fahrenheit (1,000 degrees Celsius). It is likely that early humans discovered that firing clay hardened the substance when they placed their cooking bowls over fires. As time went by, they must have realized that the fire was hardening the bottom of the vessel, and, from there, they began exploring with firing them in rudimentary kilns that were dug into the ground. This early pottery was also mainly undecorated. If there was some decoration, it was monochrome in nature or sometimes included simple linear or geometric themes.

Around 7,000 BCE, people were using a type of volcanic glass called obsidian for making sharp tools. So, they were familiar with glass, but it wouldn't be for another 2,000 years that they were able to produce glass thanks to another happy accident. Pliny, a Roman historian, wrote about the discovery of the first man-made glass around 5,000 BCE. It happened when Phoenician merchants placed their pots for cooking on rocks rich in sodium near a fire. The fire melted those sodium-rich rocks, and, in the process, the melted rock material was mixed with sand. This resulted in molten glass.

While archaeologists can neither confirm nor deny Pliny's account, they have discovered glass beads in Mesopotamia and Egypt that date to around 3,500 BCE. With the discovery of a way to produce glass, it became possible to apply glazes to pottery. Glazed pottery began to be produced in Mesopotamia at the beginning of the Bronze Age (3,000 BCE), but it wasn't until 1,500 BCE that Egyptians began to build factories for creating glassware to hold oils and ointments.

Another breakthrough moment occurred around 3,500 BCE when the pottery wheel was invented. That allows potters to make ceramics with radial symmetry. After this, we also see an evolution in pottery decoration. It begins with elaborate paintings that made many ceramic pieces into genuine works of art. At this time, the decorations involved using an oxidizing and reducing atmosphere during the firing process. This allowed them to achieve some special effects that are most evident in the Greek Attic vases made during the 6th and 5th centuries BCE.

Right up until the 16th century CE (common era--synonymous with AD), the main type of ceramic product was earthenware which was mostly manufactured in Europe and the Middle East. In the 4th century CE, the Chinese introduced the first high-temperature kilns that could reach heats up to 2462 degrees Fahrenheit (1350 degrees Celsius). By 600 CE, they also developed porcelain, which is a material that has less than a one percent porosity made with kaolin clay. These technologies were diffused during the Middle Ages as trade via the Silk Road, and the porcelain technology spread throughout Islamic countries and Europe because of the travels of Marco Polo.

In the 15th century, ironworkers in Europe developed the earliest blast furnaces that could reach temperatures as high as 2732 degrees Fahrenheit (1,500 degrees Celsius). These were first used for melting iron, and they were made from natural materials. In the 16th century, synthetic materials were developed with better resistance to high temperatures. With that, the industrial revolution was born.

Since that time, the ceramic industry has undergone profound transformation. The production of traditional ceramics and glass has become ubiquitous. Moreover, new products that take advantage of ceramic properties like low thermal and electrical conductivity, as well as high chemical resistance and melting points, have been developed. In 1850, the era of technical ceramics was born with the introduction of the first porcelain electrical insulators.

The products from ceramic and glass industries have been important contributors to growth in numerous technologically advanced fields such as electronics, medical, energy, automotive, and space exploration. Ceramics also allow for the creation of materials that have tailored properties to meet very specific requirements for customized applications. These include things like nanotechnology that allows for new materials, and products like transparent and ductile ceramics and microscopic capacitors.

History of Glazes

Relatively speaking, the history of glazing ceramics developed more slowly since not only did the appropriate materials need to be discovered, but the firing technology also had to advance to the point where a kiln could reach the temperatures necessary in a reliable manner. The first glazes that have been documented date to the 4th millennium BCE. The earliest style known is that of Egyptian faience, which is a sintered-quartz ceramic. It differs from tin-glazed pottery referred to as faience today. The Egyptian sintering process heated quartz which underwent vitrification to form bright and lustrous colors. It is a similar process to that of stonepaste or fritware found in the Middle East. While Egyptian faience contains the elements of glass, it is not considered glass in the proper sense.

The Egyptian faience technique was usually applied to small objects, and these were found in a variety of contexts, including tombs. While this was a widely-used precursor to glazing, glazing on true pottery didn't happen until the invention of glass in approximately 1,500 BCE. This occurred in the Middle East and Egypt, and the first glazes were ash glazes, and in China, glazes that used feldspar. Lead glazing became widespread in many areas of the Old World by 100 BCE.

Glazed brick dates to the 13th century BCE, where it is found at the Elamite Temple at the Iranian archaeological site of Chogha Zanbil. There is also an early glazed brick structure, known as the Iron Pagoda. This was built in 1049 CE in China. Lead-glazed earthenware is seen during the Warring States Period--475 to 221

BCE--in China. Prior to the use of earthenware, glaze was applied to stoneware around 1,600 BCE.

Ash glazes were seen during the Kofun period (300 - 538 CE) in Japan, and around 552 to 794 CE, there were various colors being produced. By this time, natural ash glazes were being used throughout Japan. By the 13th century CE, flower designs were painted with blue, red, yellow, green, and black overglazes, which were very popular because of the appearance they produced on the ceramics.

Glazed ceramics became very prevalent in Islamic pottery and art from the 8th century CE onward. Islamic potters developed a new glazing technology called tin-opacified glazing. This produces a glaze that is white, glossy, and opaque. Early Islamic opaque glazes are found on blue-painted ceramics in Basra. These also date to the 8th century CE. In Iraq in the 9th century CE, stoneware was developed.

Ceramic pots are classified with respect to the temperature at which they have been fired. Earthenware pots are fired at temperatures between 1,832 degrees Fahrenheit (1,000 degrees Celsius) and 2,102 degrees Fahrenheit (1,150 degrees Celsius). Stoneware and porcelain, on the other hand, are fired at temperatures greater than 2,192 degrees Fahrenheit (1,200 degrees Celsius). In each case, the composition of the clay must be correct so that when it reaches what is called the 'maturing temperature,' it begins to vitrify--transform into glass. The partial melting of certain components is what provides the 'glue' that gives the ceramic its strength.

With regard to glazes, they must include what is called a ceramic flux to lower the melting point of glass formers such as silica and boron trioxide. Fluxes are usually oxides, and the most common ones contain lead, sodium, lithium, calcium, potassium, magnesium, zinc, strontium, barium, and manganese. To modify the visual appearance, colorants like iron oxide are also included. The production of this glass glaze acts as a sealant for earthenware ceramics. Earthenware is porous. Over time, liquid that gets soaked into it will eventually leak through. That's why the innovation of glazing was such an important breakthrough in the production of ceramics.

Nowadays, and for the last several centuries, most pottery produced has been and continues to be glazed. There are some styles, like terracotta, for example, that are not glazed, but if used architecturally, even terracotta will be glazed. Glazed brick has also become very common, and you'll even find various types of ceramic glazes in places like insulators for overhead power lines. Glazes tend to be named after the main fluxing agent, and the most important of the traditional glaze groups are the following:

- **Ash Glaze**: It is made from wood or plant ash and contains lime and potash. It is important in East Asia.

- **Lead Glazes**: These can be plain or colored, and they are transparent and shiny after being fired. They can be fired at lower temperatures--1,470 degrees Fahrenheit (800 degrees Celsius). These have been used in China for around 2,000 years.

- **Feldspathic**: These are the glazes for porcelain. They crystallize from volcanic magma as intrusive or extrusive igneous rock.

- **Salt Glaze**: These simply use ordinary salt and are mostly applied to European stoneware.

- **Tin Glaze**: This involves the use of lead glaze that is made opaque and white by adding tin. It was an important innovation among Islamic potters and is widely known in the Ancient Near East. From there, it spread to Europe, and the examples include Italian Renaissance maiolica or majolica, faience, Delftware, and Hispano-Moresque ware.

These are the traditional categories of glaze, but modern technology has resulted in the invention of new vitreous glazes that form different categories.

Glaze Colors and Decoration

There are typically two applications of glaze. One is called an underglaze that gets applied first to the 'raw,' or unfired, pottery. You can also apply an underglaze to what is called a 'biscuit' fired vessel. This is a kind of initial firing that is done for some ceramics. Once the vessel is decorated, a wet underglaze is applied over the top of it. The pigments used for the decoration fuse with the glaze, which makes it appear as though the decoration is underneath a clear layer of glaze. Blue and white porcelain is a great example of underglaze decoration.

The blue and white porcelain underglaze technique was first produced in China, but it then quickly spread to other countries. Cobalt, in the form of cobalt oxide or cobalt carbonate, is used to produce that striking blue color. After the English invention of white-bodied earthenwares like creamware in the 18th century CE, underglaze decoration became very common.

Overglaze decoration is another type of glazing. As the name implies, it is applied over the top of a layer of glaze that has already been fired. It typically uses colors in 'enamel,' which must then be fired a second time at low temperatures to fuse the color to the glaze. This use of low temperatures means that a wide range of pigments can be used. These overglaze colors are what gives ceramics a glassy, more decorative appearance. The process involves an initial firing, called the glost firing, and then the overglaze decoration is applied. Once applied, the vessel is fired again, and when it is taken out of the kiln, it has a smoother texture produced by the glaze.

Other methods include inglaze, which involves applying the paints onto the glaze before the vessel is fired. That causes the decoration to be incorporated into the glaze when it is fired. It's a great technique for tin-glazed pottery like majolica, but the range of colors that can be used is limited because they can't withstand the glost firing like an underglaze can. Mixing the pigments into the liquid glaze before firing has mostly been used to give a single color to the entire vessel. But it can also be used for creating contrasting colors as seen in the Chinese sancai--or three-color--wares.

Throughout history, many styles, like Japanese Imari ware, also combine the techniques for decorations. They might, for example, do a glost firing for the body, followed by an underglaze decoration, glaze application, and the application of overglaze enamels, after which the vessel then goes through a second firing.

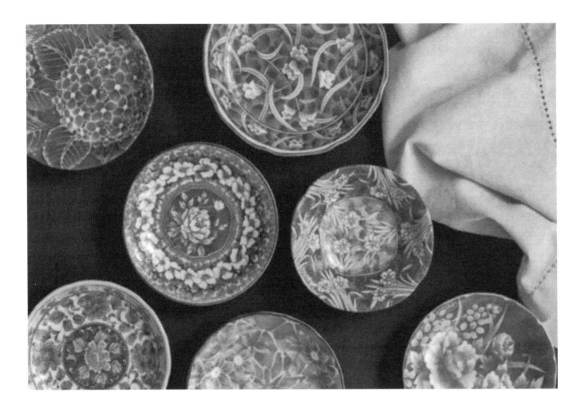

The importance of ceramics and glazes to human history and progress cannot be overstated. These innovations have made a huge difference in the advancement of human populations and their technological inventions over time. It ranks among the first instances of humans learning to manipulate different materials to produce a variety of useful tools. The development of ceramics and ceramic techniques like glazing have contributed to our ability to store foods and other items, and has allowed us to accumulate resources for long-term use.

That is one of the hallmarks of human success, the ability to store resources. It allowed for exponential population growth as well as for specialization in professions as well as food production. Because we were able to store the food we weren't ready to eat, we could produce a surplus. That meant that we could store food so that some people could do things other than those tasks related to food production. This, in turn, meant we could begin to develop other technologies and make cultural advances. And all of this thanks to a relatively humble technology like the production of ceramics!

This is the value of making ceramics and producing ceramic glazes. You are truly entering a fascinating area, one that can be a satisfying hobby or a fulfilling career. Before we get into the specifics of ceramic glazing and firing techniques, it's important to have a good understanding of the science behind glazes and the benefits of applying them. We'll take a look at that next.

Chapter Summary

In this chapter, we've discussed the history of ceramics and glazing techniques. Specifically, we've discussed the following topics:

- The earliest ceramics;

- The Venus figurines;

- The discovery of firing techniques;

- The history of glazes;

- The different types of glazes;

- Glaze decorations and colors.

In the next chapter, you will learn all about the science and benefits of glazing.

Chapter Two: The Science and Benefits of Glaze

Glazes really changed how pottery could be used and how it looks as well. Glaze can serve a number of purposes, and there is a science to how various glazes were developed. Let's begin by taking a look at why it's helpful to glaze a pot.

Benefits of Glazing

One of the most important benefits of applying a glaze, particularly to earthenware vessels, is that it makes them suitable for holding liquids. Unglazed biscuit earthenware is inherently porous, and, over time, water will seep into those porosities and cause leaks. Glazing seals those porosities, and it also gives the vessel a tougher surface.

Glazes can also be applied to stoneware and porcelain, as well as earthenware. On all of these types of vessels, glazes can help to form different surface finishes. These include matte or glossy finishes, and, of course, glazes can add color. They can also help to enhance any underlying designs or textures such as inscribed, carved, or painted designs.

Finally, glazes increase the compressive strength of a ceramic body. That just means it makes the vessel more able to resist breaking when placed under compression. So, you can see that applying a glaze gives pottery a lot of advantages, but let's examine the science of how they are developed.

The Science Behind Glazes

Glazes can be categorized in a couple of ways. First, they may be classified with respect to how they're produced--either they are vitrified or crystallized.

Vitrification: This is a process by which the clay is fired to hotter and hotter temperatures until it reaches a point where, as it cools, it will increase in strength and density. When it has reached the point where it is dense enough and strong enough to do what it is intended to do, it is called 'mature.' The point at which it is mature depends on the material. For example, buff stoneware is mature when it has attained a 1.5 percent porosity, whereas hard porcelain is considered vitreous at zero percent porosity, and terracotta requires a 3 to 5 percent porosity to be considered vitreous. You can run into problems, however, if you fire a vessel body to higher and higher degrees of vitrification because that can cause problems like warping and blistering. For that reason, for many types of wares, semi-vitreous is considered strong and durable enough, particularly if the glaze fits the ware well and is itself hard and durable.

Crystalline glazes: Through the process of producing this kind of glaze, large multi-colored crystals are produced on a super-gloss, low alumina glaze through several holds and soaks during cooling. What does that mean? Well, during the cooling process for many kinds of glazes, very large crystals will form that either completely cover the glaze or are more widely scattered. For instance, matte glazes are the result of a dense mesh of crystals that are 'growing' on its surface. It is possible to get unwanted crystals, but the term crystalline means that you are trying to produce these large macro crystals.

A nice effect of these crystals is that they often appear to be floating on the glaze, and, additionally, they will wrap around to match the vessel's contour. They can be very large and beautiful with an infinite variety of shapes, colors, and patterns. But, for that to happen, they need the right conditions. Glazes that will crystallize have a 'zone of crystallization.' If you want to get the best results, you'll have to slow the firing at the peak of that zone in order to ensure that all of the glaze materials are dissolved. Then, you cool it to where the material that forms crystals precipitates out. When you reach that point, you hold the temperature so that the crystals will grow. That's why you'll need an accurate electronic kiln controller, particularly if you'll be doing this repeatedly. In fact, the best producer of crystalline glazes will often do hundreds or even thousands of firings while they carefully record their recipes, schedules, and procedures.

Temperature Classifications

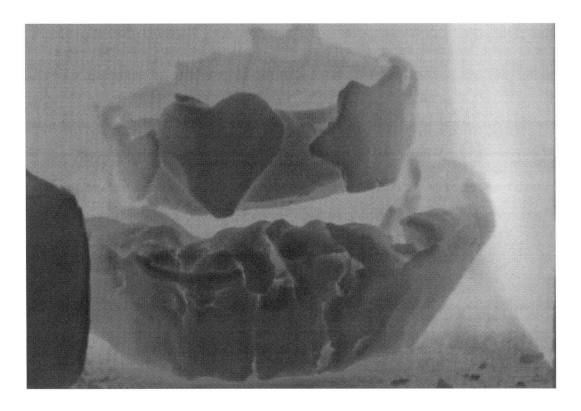

Glazes are also classified in accordance with their firing temperature.

High Temperature Glazes: These are glazes for which firing temperatures are between 2,192 degrees Fahrenheit (1,200 degrees Celsius) and 2,552 degrees Fahrenheit (1,400 degrees Celsius). High temperature glazes are used for ceramics like bone-china, bone-porcelain, and electro ceramics. They are also used for fireclay products.

Medium Temperature Glazes: These are glazes that are fired at temperatures between 1,832 degrees Fahrenheit (1,000 degrees Celsius) and 1,922 degrees Fahrenheit (1,050 degrees Celsius). Medium temperature glazes are most often used for things like earthenware bodies that will be used as tableware, sanitary wares, tiles, and the like.

Low Temperature Glazes: These are glazes that are fired at temperatures between 1,800 degrees Fahrenheit (982 degrees Celsius) and 2,000 degrees Fahrenheit (1,093 degrees Celsius). These are typically used for things like majolica, where the body is very porous.

Glaze Composition

In order to cover the entire surface of the vessel with the glaze in an even fashion, it's important that the surface tension be correct. The glaze composition is important for that, and it again depends on what kind of ceramics you're working with. You want the glaze to hinder the shrinkage of the vessel body. For porcelain bodies, glazes high in calcium, strontium, barium, or beryllium and colored with chromium, iron, and cobalt all work well for hindering body shrinkage. Likewise, glazes with a high content of calcined kaolin, alumina, or other fill materials work well, but the maximum effect that helps prevent distortion created by body shrinkage is obtained with chromium and calcium glazes. The highest amount of body shrinkages is found with glazes that contain feldspath and magnesia.

Another important factor in formulating glaze composition is that you don't want it to be water- soluble. The reason is that when a slip is applied to the vessel, the soluble part of that penetrates and acts as a flux which will deprive the main glaze of the constituents it needs to work properly. Glaze slips can contain some water-soluble material, but it shouldn't be entirely water-soluble.

Glazes usually contain three main ingredients to achieve the viscosity needed, lower the melting point of the glaze mixture, and support the vessel body. These ingredients and their functions are as follows:

1. **Silicon dioxide**: this is provided to the main body to help decrease porosity;
2. **Aluminum oxide**: This is useful for enhancing the viscosity, or thickness, of the glaze, and it does that via crosslinked silica networks;
3. **Fluxes**: These are typically alkaline earth metal oxides, and they help lower the mixture's melting point to the firing temperature.

Other common components of a glaze are transition metal oxides. These are oxygen atoms that bind to transition metals. In a glaze, they provide color.

Properties of Glaze

There are three properties of glaze that are particularly important for potters. These three are the color, the opacity (clearness), and the texture (rough or smooth) of the glaze. The latter two should be considered with respect to the melting properties of solid mixtures. As you increase the temperature in a kiln, the amount of solid material in your glaze mixture diminishes while the proportion of liquid increases. If you want to achieve a smooth, shiny surface, you'll need to melt all of the solid material by heating the glaze to a higher, 'maturing' temperature.

If you want glaze that is opaque and with a smooth surface, you'll need some solid matter left to scatter light. That means you'll heat the glaze to a lower temperature than the maturing temperature. The exact temperature depends on your glaze mixture.

Finally, if you want a glaze that is slightly rough, you'll want it to mainly still be composed of solid material with a smaller portion of melted ingredients. In fact, you want just enough liquid to stick the components together and to the vessel. These types of vessels are not recommended to be used for holding food.

This is, of course, a gross oversimplification since most glazes are composed of many components, but I think, by now, you get the general idea. For most glazes, the situation is far more complicated, but these are the main considerations for texture and opacity. What about color?

The third property of glazes is color, but most of the major minerals found in glazes are colorless, so how do you vary the color? Quartz and corundum, two components of glazes, are found in nature as white, crystalline solids if they are in their pure state. If they are contaminated, however, they come in different forms. Amethyst and citrine are quartz that has been contaminated with iron, whereas ruby is corundum that is contaminated with chromium. Sapphire colors are the result of corundum that is contaminated with iron, cobalt, titanium, and vanadium.

Therefore, for most glazes, the color is the result of oxides that are what are referred to as first row transition metals. This is a phrase used in chemistry that refers to the atomic structure of these metals. In addition to the ones mentioned above, copper is another first row transition metal that is widely used. In fact, for coloring pottery, iron, copper, and cobalt are the three most common oxides used. Of these three, iron is the most versatile. It can produce yellow, red, brown, blue, and green colors in several different shades.

For producing color, the two most important variables are the oxidation state and the environment for the transition metal ion. If you're using a kiln that is heated with gas, wood, or oil, you can use reducing conditions during the firing process. This is where you restrict the supply of oxygen which causes the atmosphere--i.e., environment--in the kiln to become rich in carbon monoxide. Transition metals in low concentrations in your glaze will be reduced to a lower oxidation state as a result of this. That can result in many different colors. Applying some glaze with higher compositions of transition metals to parts of the vessel can also result in color variations on the same vessel.

Ways to Apply Glaze

There are certain things you want to be aware of when applying glazes. It's important so that you can achieve the effects you're hoping to get with the glaze. First, you need to clean the surface of the clay. You don't want any dust or grease that could spoil the finished appearance.

Next, you need to make sure you mix a large enough volume of glaze to accomplish your goal. You'll need to work out what is going to be a suitable thickness of glaze for your vessel. These are important decisions that do, to some extent, determine which application method you will use for the desired result. You can even use more than one method of application to achieve a special effect. With that said, let's look at the techniques you can use to apply the glaze. We'll cover these in more detail in subsequent chapters, but we'll discuss them briefly here.

Brushing

This is typically done on unfired vessels called greenware. It's typically used for vessels that will only be fired once or if you're trying to achieve a brushed appearance. You can use a variety of different brushes, including soft hair watercolor brushes or even house painting brushes. If you really want to get into the details, you can even make your own brush from animal hair.

Brushing will result in a streaky appearance typically, but if that is not what you want, you can use Chinese brushes that use several bamboo shafts to produce a 6-inch wide soft brush. This kind of brush will not produce the typical streaky appearance, but you will have to cover the large parts of the vessel in one sweep since you can't avoid the streaks if you have to go back over it numerous times. You can also use a glaze that is so liquidy that it disguises the brush marks. If you want to end up with a flat surface, brushing is probably not the ideal way to go.

Dipping

Dipping is another technique you can use for glaze application. It involves dipping the vessel into a bucket of glaze to achieve a coating that is of even thickness. It's the most useful technique when speed and efficiency are more important. That being said, one of the problems you can have with this technique is if the glaze starts to run. If that does happen, you can remove it with a knife to make sure the surface is smooth. You will have to touch up the spots where you held the vessel when you dipped it, and this can be done using a brush or your fingers.

Pouring

This is a technique that is often done in conjunction with dipping on the same vessel. The inside might be poured, for example, while the outside is dipped. Pouring can be done with various tools, such as a pitcher, can, or even a ladle, but the quality of flow will depend on the pouring vessel you use. Aluminum pouring vessels with narrow spouts often work well.

When preparing the glaze for a pour, you want it to be slightly thinner than what you would use for dipping since you will likely overlap poured glaze with dipped glaze, and too much results in running. Pouring can achieve numerous decorative effects, such as overlapping glazes of different properties or colors.

Spraying

Spraying is a very useful application technique, but it does take some experience to get an even coating and to judge the right thickness of the glaze to cover the vessel adequately. You can use this technique for the whole piece or for just applying glaze to certain areas of the vessel. This technique does require some specialized equipment like an atomizer, though a garden hose sprayer can be used for this purpose. There are also small spray units that use containers of freon gas, or you can also use a vacuum cleaner with reversible air controls. Some spray guns require a compressor for controlling the air, and for small applications, you can use an airbrush for this purpose. Many of these sprayers are relatively expensive, but when you're doing detailed work, particularly if you're working with overglazes, these are indispensable.

When you are working with a spray gun to apply glaze, it will produce floating glaze dust in the atmosphere. You'll need to take the appropriate safety precautions since the colorants are toxic. You'll want to wear a respirator and do your spraying in an appropriately ventilated space. Additionally, the glaze materials are abrasive and will cause wear to the nozzles of the guns. To help with that, you can use carbide spray tips, and you should clean the equipment carefully after each use. Glazes will typically cause the most damage to airbrushes since the glaze materials are not as finely ground as paints, lusters, or enamels. If you need to use an airbrush, you'll likely find it has problems with clogging.

The glazes you use for spraying should be thinner in consistency than with other application methods. You might also want to add in a deflocculant, like one percent sodium silicate solution, to minimize the water content in the glaze and lower the likelihood of excessively wetting the vessel. It also helps prevent the washing of wet glaze from the surface. Because the glaze is thinner, it will take several coatings to get the desired result. It can help to place the vessel on a banding wheel to spray it.

A big disadvantage of this technique is that it wastes material. For that reason, you might think about implementing a system to retrieve some of the wasted materials, particularly if they're expensive. You'll also want to use masking techniques like latex or paper if you're trying to create an intricate pattern.

Stippling

This is done with the edge or tip of a brush, or it can also be done using a sponge. If you want a broken texture, this is the technique to use, and the best brushes are house painting brushes or artist's brushes typically used for oil painting. You'll have to be careful about the amount of glaze you charge into the brush because it can run out.

Spattering

This is a kind of spraying technique, but it's one where the tool used creates a broken, uneven spray. Sometimes you can achieve this effect accidentally if your spray gun is worn out. Typically, you'll use a toothbrush or some other form of stiff-bristled brush. You dip that into glaze and then hold it near the area you'll be spraying. You can then pull a knife blade across the bristles so that they are bent away from the work. Then, you simply let go, and it springs back to create the uneven sprayed appearance.

Sponging

Sponges are a great artistic tool for creating interesting textures. You can use either natural or synthetic sponges to soak up glaze and apply it to the vessel. You can cut synthetic sponges or even burn them to create different patterns. This is an excellent way to create a repeating pattern on the vessel in a fast, efficient manner. You can also get delicate patterns as long as your sponge is finely grained, and you can create overlapping sponge marks or stamps to create depth to the decoration. While the sponge will deteriorate, it can last quite a long time if you wash it carefully after each use.

Trailing

This is a useful technique for creating linear designs on the ceramic piece. It can be produced with numerous tools such as a plastic, squeezable bottle with a small opening at the tip. You can also make a simple tool from two pieces of bamboo. The glazes used for this technique are best if they are thicker than normal in their consistency. That's because trailed glazes tend to flatten down and spread during firing. If you want to produce a detailed drawing, you might want to consider trailing the glaze on an unfired or bisque-fired surface before applying the main glaze. That's because trailed glazes can be fragile during handling; it's easy to knock off a raised portion of the trailed glaze. If you really need the detail of a drawing to be maintained through firing, it might be better to use a different technique like brushing or underglaze pencils.

Applying Multiple Glazes

This is different from using multiple firing processes for different glazes. This actually refers to applying two or more glazes over each other in different ways to achieve a specific result. You typically will use similar glaze bases for these multiple applications because they will melt in a similar way during firing. It is possible, however, to apply different glaze bases and achieve rich results.

If you're applying multiple glazes, it's important to remember that the work needs to be done in a short span of time so that one glaze won't dry out before you apply the next. If it does dry, the glaze might flake off or 'crawl.' If it crawls, that will result in a lizard skin pattern, and that frequently occurs when you apply a glaze with a high clay content over the top of one with a low clay content. As the second glaze begins to dry, greater shrinkage occurs, and that creates places for crawling to happen.

Glazes used with multiple applications are typically thinner than normal consistency. But if you want to achieve a certain effect from excessive running or a thick buildup of low-flowing glaze, then you can make them normal consistency or even thicker. Be aware, however, that if the glazes become too thick, you will have problems with running.

Chapter Summary

In this chapter, we've discussed the benefits of applying glaze and the science behind how glazes are made. Specifically, we've covered the following topics:

- The benefits of glaze application;

- Vitrification and crystalline glazes;

- Temperature classifications;

- Glaze composition;

- The properties of glaze;

- Ways to apply glaze.

In the next chapter, you will learn all about the equipment you'll need for glazing.

Chapter Three: Equipment for Glazing

As with any task you need to do, you need the right equipment to do it correctly. What's more, you want to have everything ready so that you're not obliged to call a halt in the middle of a project to find a piece of equipment you need. For glazing, the tools you need can be separated according to the following categories:

- Safety Equipment;

- Glaze Preparation Tools;

- Glazing Work Surfaces;

- Glaze Application Tools;

- Glaze Firing Equipment;

- Glaze Removal Tools.

Let's take a closer look at the tools in each category.

Safety Equipment

There are a number of dangers that you can be exposed to when glazing, and, of course, you'll want to take appropriate measures to protect your clothing. The basic safety equipment you'll need includes an apron, mask, gloves, and safety goggles.

Apron: This will help to keep your clothing protected from dirt, and most aprons are equipped with pockets that are very convenient for storing other tools. There are several styles of apron, but a split-leg design with adjustable leg straps will keep the front of your body well-shielded. It's also a good idea to get one that's flame-resistant since you'll be working around a kiln.

Mask: Wearing a mask is vital for protecting your lungs from inhaled dust from clay and glaze and from the glaze spray mists. You should wear a mask any time you're sanding or grinding off glaze or mixing dry glaze. Additionally, you should wear it when you're spraying a fine mist of glaze.

Gloves: You'll also need to protect your hands from the glaze. By wearing gloves, you'll avoid getting the oil from your hands on your ceramics. Even the small amount of natural oil that is on your hands can prevent the glaze from properly attaching to some types of ceramics like bisque ware. You can keep disposable gloves in your studio, but you'll also want a pair of thick, heat-resistant gloves for unloading your kiln and when you're handling sharp objects such as broken pottery.

Safety Goggles: Whenever you're doing this kind of work, you must protect your eyes from harm and the irritation that can result from dust particles. You should always wear goggles when you're mixing dry glaze, spraying glaze, and when you're sanding or grinding to remove excess glaze or so-called cookies.

Glaze Preparation Tools

Once you have all of your safety equipment ready to go, you'll want to get together the tools you'll need for preparing your glaze. At this point, you'll need to have your ceramic objects ready for glazing as well. As with the safety equipment, you should have all of the tools handy, so you don't have to look for something at a critical moment in the process. Here's a list of what you'll require for this step.

Sponges: These will be used for wiping your ceramic clean. You'll need it to be clear and free from any kind of dust or lint particles prior to applying the glaze. If you don't have it cleaned properly, the glaze won't adhere as it should to the object. You'll be wiping the ceramic down frequently throughout the process, so you'll want to have several sponges ready for use. If you've been working with ceramics at all, you'll likely already have several of these around since they are useful for a number of reasons. For glazing, you'll be using them to both apply and decorate the glaze so that you'll get a unique result. We'll cover this in more depth in a subsequent chapter.

Wax Resist: Wax resist refers to a liquid wax emulsion that you use to keep the glaze from sticking to particular parts of the ceramic.

For example, with bisque ware, you'll need to coat the base of the ceramic so that it won't stick to the shelf of the kiln when it's being fired. You'll also apply wax resist to areas of the ceramic that will come into contact with other ceramic vessels during firing. This can easily happen with lid rims, for example. Lastly, you can also use wax resist to decorate your ceramic vessel. You can apply it using a brush to those areas where you'll be doing something different with the decoration.

Glaze Supplies: These include things like the glaze and various additives. You can either buy a glaze that has already been prepared from a ceramics store, or you can prepare your own. If you're preparing your own, you'll need the following supplies:

- **Glazes and underglazes**--These are the main decorating ingredients in glazing. You can purchase them in different colors and with different properties depending on the result you want to achieve. These could be a matte finish, a shiny glaze, or a flat appearance. You also will make your choice of glazes depending on the use of the vessel. As an example, if you're planning on using it for holding food, you'll require the glazes and underglazes you choose to be food-safe.

- **Suspendaid**--This is used for thinning out any glaze you're brushing onto the vessel. It will make it more like the consistency of a dipping glaze. It's a great additive that also prevents the settling of the glaze.

Glaze Measuring Tools: These include things like a scale, spoons, and cups. First, you'll need a measuring cup. You'll use this for measuring out the glaze and any additives you're using. You'll want to choose a sturdy cup with clear markings that will hold up over time.

You'll also need measuring spoons, and it's a good idea to have a set of different sizes. That way, it will be much easier to measure and mix small portions of glaze additives. It's a good idea to get metal spoons since the size of the spoon is engraved on the handle. That way, you don't have to worry about the size fading or becoming illegible.

Another handing glaze measuring tool is a scoop. It can assist with measuring, particularly dry glazes and dry glaze ingredients. A clear one that is at least six ounces works well for this purpose. Finally, you'll need a scale that can measure out specific amounts of something like dry glaze. You can even use this for measuring the specific gravity of your glaze mixture, something we'll talk more about in subsequent chapters. For this purpose, a digital scale works best, but make sure you get an accurate one.

Glaze Mixing Tools: These include buckets, bowls, drills, and the like. Buckets are something you've got to have in your studio. They are useful for mixing dry glaze, storing wet glaze, and dipping ceramics. Ideally, you want two to five-gallon buckets with lids you can seal. A screw-on lid works best since that can ensure it's airtight.

Bowls are helpful when you have to mix a smaller amount of glaze. You require wide, shallow bowls that will be very useful when you want to dip a smaller ceramic, such as a mug or another type of decor piece. A bowl will let you clearly see the item as you dip the sides into the glaze, whereas a bucket doesn't allow for that. Bowls are also useful for pouring techniques we'll discuss in subsequent chapters. With a bowl, you can easily pour the glaze over a ceramic piece on a rack, and you can even catch the excess for use later on.

It's also helpful to have a funnel to help with pouring the glaze. That will help prevent spilling any of the contents. Get a few in different sizes, so you're ready no matter the type and amount of glaze you're making. You'll also want a spatula for mixing, especially with small amounts of glaze. Silicone spatulas work best, particularly ones that are a single, seamless piece. They're sturdy and won't easily break. They are also easy to clean. Plus, silicone is smooth, so you won't have to worry about scratching the bowl as you scrape the glaze from the bottom and sides.

Another helpful mixing tool is a whisk. These can actually even be better than spatulas for preparing glaze. In fact, whisking can allow you to produce a more even glaze faster than a spatula. You'll also need a strainer or sieves for ensuring the glaze is smooth and even in its consistency. You'll need to pour the glaze through the strainer into a second bucket, and you'll want to use a tool to push the clumps through too. This will help you to catch debris that might be in the glaze so that it doesn't get put on the ceramic piece. For this purpose, it's good to have a set of three sieves that are different sizes. That way, you'll have the right size for any amount and type of glaze you're mixing.

The glaze mixing tool you'll want is a hydrometer. You'll use this to measure the specific gravity of the glaze after you've mixed it. It also works for slips. You'll have to check out what is the ideal specific gravity for the technique you're using to decorate your piece. By using a hydrometer, you can ensure that you get the same thickness each time you make that glaze. That makes it very convenient. The best hydrometer is one that has glass-like clarity, but it is plastic so that it is shatter-proof.

A drill with a mixing attachment can help you to produce a smooth, even glaze after mixing. It's probably better to get one that's both rechargeable and cordless for the most convenience and efficiency of use. Then, just join the drill attachment to the tip of the drill and you're ready to go. Finally, a pint bottle mixer like a handheld mixer you might use to froth milk is a great tool for creating an even, smooth consistency to your glaze.

Glazing Work Surfaces

To work in a comfortable way while creating the various glaze decorations, you'll really want to have a spacious work surface. There are a couple of things that are essential for this, including a worktable that's set at a comfortable height. You don't want to be hunched over while you work, and you don't want to have to strain to reach objects on a work surface that is too high. You can also get a lightweight, portable table so that you can set it up anywhere and store it when you're not working.

An adjustable height tabletop riser is a great work surface that, as the description says, lets you arrange its height to your preference. You just place this on top of the table you're working on, and you can glaze your pottery while standing or sitting as you might prefer. That's a great convenience when you're working for hours on a ceramic piece. If you opt for this piece of equipment, you'll want one that is easy to adjust, preferably with just one handle. You'll also want it to have a spacious work area so you can fit your vessel on it.

Another useful surface for applying glaze is a banding wheel. The surface of the wheel spins, so that makes it much easier to turn the vessel and reach all sides of your ceramic. You'll want to get a banding wheel that is well-designed and sturdy. A 12-inch diameter is a good size, but you can get smaller ones as well.

Glaze Application Tools

Once you've got your work surface and glaze prepared, it's time for applying it to your ceramic. For that, you'll need a variety of application tools like tongs, tape, brushes, and such. These can help you use a variety of decorating techniques, and they can make your work much easier too.

For dipping ceramics, you'll need dipping tongs. They will let you hold the piece in the perfect position as you dip it into the glaze. You'll also need brushes for brushing on glaze as well as for other purposes. They are an essential tool in your studio. You can use them for wax resist as well as the glaze, and you can use different types of brushes to achieve different designs.

For those finer decorations that have more detail, you'll want to use a glaze bulb applicator. It's best if this tool is made so that it's airtight to prevent your underglaze from drying out while you're in the middle of applying it. Another handy tool is a slip trailing applicator for applying decorative slips. Slip trailing allows you to create decorative lines as well as raised textures, and for that, you'll need a three and one-ounce applicator. They are lightweight, and each one comes with three tips that are of different sizes for varying your designs.

A glaze spray gun is another good tool for applying glaze and underglaze using the spray technique. To power that, you'll need an air compressor. This is a tool that creates pressurized air and then pushes it with amplified force through the spray gun. These come in a variety of sizes, but you can find a portable, lightweight, and quiet air compressor for this purpose.

It's also a good idea to have a booth for spray glazing. This is particularly important for safety reasons to contain the glaze particles created when spraying glaze on a ceramic. It will prevent them from floating throughout the room, but this does not mean that you don't have to wear your safety gear. You will still need to protect yourself with your mask, gloves, and safety goggles. You should look for a portable booth so that you can move it to wherever you're working.

Finally, you'll need some transfer or stencil paper and some masking tape. You can use the stencil and transfer papers to create more designs for decorating your ceramics. Masking tape acts as a resistor for those areas where you don't want glaze applied. This will give you the freedom to create a variety of interesting, unique patterns that reflect your personal style. You can find both of these items in many local stores, and they're a great way to expand your creativity.

Glaze Firing Equipment

Once you have your ceramic piece decorated with glaze, you're ready to fire the glaze. That requires a kiln. If you already have a kiln, you're all set but, if you don't, there are a couple of options. You might be able to rent space for your ceramics at a kiln that is available to the public if you have one near you. Firing your pieces will take minimally 24 hours to complete depending on the size of the kiln and how full it is.

Another option for a kiln if you don't already have one is to buy one. This will allow you to take your pottery hobby to the next level. You should definitely make this investment if you're thinking of going pro, but how do you know which kiln to buy? Well, there are several things to consider, and since this will be fairly sizable financial investment, it's important to consider carefully exactly what you need. Toward that end, there are several questions it would be wise to answer before purchasing a kiln so that you can find one that best suits your needs.

1. What kind of clay will you be firing?

Remember that you need a kiln that will reach the necessary temperature to cause the clay to mature. The temperature range of your kiln will vary, and you need different temperatures for the type of material--earthenware, stoneware, porcelain, or glass.

2. What kind of glaze are you using?

Just like with clay, glazes don't melt at the same temperature. Some glazes, such as Raku, need a lower temperature, but others, such as oxide stains, need higher temperatures. You want to make sure you purchase a kiln that will do what you need it to do temperature-wise.

3. What sizes of pieces do you want to create and how many?

Obviously, it's important to get the right size kiln for your needs. If you're hoping to go pro, you'll probably need a larger size to accommodate more pieces, but if you're just doing this as a hobby, you can get by with a smaller size.

4. How big is the place where you'll be keeping the kiln?

You have to consider the size of the space where you plan to house the kiln. You should take measurements of the height, length, and width to ensure that you can fit the kiln itself and allow for a minimum of two feet on every side of the kiln for breathing room.

5. How much power is available for the kiln?

If you're getting a larger kiln, it will require more energy to run it. You'll want to match the amperage and voltage requirements of the kiln with what you have available in the space where you'll be housing it. If you need a kiln with higher energy requirements, you might have to invest more in the installation process.

Answering these questions will help you decide which kiln to buy, but there are a few other considerations as well. When you're searching for the perfect kiln for you, you'll need to consider the size of it. This is dependent, in part, on the types of projects you want to do, but there are a variety of sizes of kilns available.

- **Smaller kilns**: These measure up to 9 inches by 11 inches and are great for firing beads, small ceramic pieces, doll parts, and test items. These are probably a better choice for beginners.

- **Medium kilns**: These measure 18 by 18 inches, and are recommended for those interested in firing larger pieces such as pots, bowls, and plates, but are not planning on firing large numbers of pieces. You can, however, fire multiple small pieces in a kiln this size.

- **Large kilns**: These measure up to 29 inches by 27 inches, although a 23 inch by 27-inch kiln is the most common size of kiln purchased. It is intended for the average potter, but the larger size is recommended for production use.

While the size of the kiln is important, it's also critical to think about what you'll be firing and how often. You want to fire a full kiln since that's the best way to achieve maximum efficiency. For that reason, you also want to consider how long it will take to fill the size kiln you're thinking of buying.

Electricity and Voltage Requirements

This is another important factor to consider when buying a kiln. The normal voltage for most households is 120V. If you're thinking of getting a smaller kiln, this won't be a problem, but larger kilns will frequently require 240V. It can be a good idea to consult with an electrician to ensure you have the proper connections.

Additionally, you'll want to ensure that you have the appropriate breakers for the amperage requirements of your kiln. To determine the amps you have available, check inside the fuse/breaker box of the plug you're planning on using. There is a number that indicates the amperage. For most US homes, they are protected by 15 - 20 amp breakers, but some of the larger kilns require 60 amp breakers. Without the correct amp number, your kiln won't work.

Temperature and Cone

Temperature is a very important factor for deciding on the kiln that's right for you. This depends on the types of glazes and clays you plan to work with since some require high temperatures, whereas other materials need medium-high or medium-low temperatures.

- **Low-Fire Materials**: These include things like glass and earthenware.

- **Mid to High-Firing Materials**: Stoneware can require either mid-firing temperatures or high-firing temperatures. Porcelain requires the highest temperatures.

You want to buy a kiln that actually exceeds the maximum temperatures you will need for what you're working on. That's important since, over time, a kiln's power is reduced, which reduces its ability to hold a high temperature. Ideally, you should overestimate the temperature by some 200 - 300 degrees Fahrenheit.

If you've looked at different kilns at all, you might have seen that some models measure temperature using 'cones.' A cone differs from a Fahrenheit degree in that it measures temperature over time, and it also measures energy. Low cone temperatures will be represented with a 0 in front of other numbers. For example, you might see 018 or 019 to indicate a low cone temperature. Higher cone temperatures are two-digit numbers such as 13 or 14. The lowest cone temperature is 022 and the highest is 15. Check your materials and glazes to get their cone temperature.

Price

Of course, price is an important factor when purchasing a kiln, and their prices can vary from around $300 to closer to $4,000. While you might want to save money, if you're thinking of going pro with this hobby, you might want to invest in a good kiln since it will be worth the money you pay over time.

Top Loading or Front Loading

This might seem like a minor consideration, but you should consider your own height and back health when you're making this decision. Top loading kilns are cheaper, but if you're not tall enough, they can make your work more difficult. You can always use a stook, but you still have to lift your ceramics, and, over time, that puts a strain on your back. Front loading kilns are more expensive, but they are also more convenient, and they can save you from those back pains.

Controller Type

There are different types of controllers for most kilns. You can get a manual control that gives you the most experience when you're firing objects, but it also means you'll have to start the kiln at the lowest setting and then make all the changes throughout the entire process. You can also get controllers that give you a choice between different temperature programs, and still others that allow you to select both the cone and firing speed.

You can also get more precise controllers that have touchscreens and ensure precise firing. These also include a WiFi connection so that you can develop and edit firing programs. Many will also allow you to store various programs and make adjustments during the firing process.

Kiln Accessories

There are some accessories you'll also want to consider with the purchase of your kiln. These include various types of kiln furniture as well as racks and bricks.

- **Kiln shelves**: These are for installing in the kiln, and they need to be able to withstand repeated fires at high temperatures and cones. Typically, the shelves made of silica and alumina can withstand cone 10. If you need to fire at higher cones, there are high alumina kiln shelves that withstand the temperatures of cone 11. You can also get silicon carbide shelves which are more lightweight and thinner, and they won't warp at high temperatures.

As you might expect, however, they cost about twice as much as the other type of shelves.

- **Kiln stilts**: These are for holding and protecting the edges of your pieces when you're firing them in the low to medium-low range. Some stilts can withstand cone 10, but most of them are better used for temperatures at or below cone 6.

- **Kiln posts**: These support the shelves and allow you to optimize the space inside your kiln. They come in different levels of thickness and height.

- **Furniture kits**: You can often buy things like posts and shelves along with heat-resistant gloves and cleaning equipment in a kit. That way, you can acquire everything you need at once.

- **Bead racks**: These will also help save you space when you're firing beads, buttons, and other types of small, hanging pieces. Jewelers and potters benefit from the tool if they're making wearable ceramics.

- **Bricks**: Bricks are used as an insulator. You line the inside of the kiln with them, and they come in various shapes. They are made of two main types of material: hard bricks are great for structural support since they are strong and dense. Soft bricks retain heat more effectively, but they can't withstand higher temperatures.

Glaze Removal Tools

Once you've fired your glaze, you now need to put the final touches on your ceramic piece. For that, you're going to need to grind and smooth it out. To do that, you'll need a wheel attachment grinding stone. It will help you smooth out the bottom of your ceramic. You'll likely want one of these with a diamond grit that has a higher hardness rating. Using this tool requires that you take all safety precautions, such as wearing goggles. You should also use water with the stone to maximize its life and minimize dust.

Another good glaze removal tool is a removal grinder. It's perfect for removing sharp edges from your ceramic pieces. You can remove cookies and grind off the excess glaze on the bottom of the piece. A handheld rotary tool is very convenient and simple to use for this purpose. Most of these are also very safe and comfortable to use.

As you're probably coming to realize, working with pottery requires a rather large collection of tools that are used for a variety of purposes. It's important to consider your goals as you look for the kinds of tools and supplies that will best suit your needs. You want the tools you use to be effective, convenient, and safe for what you're doing. Even if you're just doing this as a hobby, make sure that you don't skimp on the tools you need. There are less expensive choices you can make, but be sure you don't sacrifice safety for price. You're doing this, after all, because you enjoy it, and you want to keep it that way.

Chapter Summary

In this chapter, we've discussed the various types of equipment you'll need for glazing pottery. Specifically, we've covered the following topics:

- The types of safety equipment you need;

- Tools for preparing glazes and the work surfaces for applying them;

- The tools you'll need to apply glazes;

- The types of kilns and what they work best for;

- The tools to remove excess glaze and polish your piece.

In the next chapter, you will learn all about the different types of glazes.

Chapter Four: Types of Glazes

While glazing your pottery simply means you're covering it in glass, there is more to it than that. There are many different things to consider when choosing a pottery glaze. Clearly, you want beautiful results, but getting what you want means taking a number of things into consideration, including the temperature you will use for firing, the use of the ceramic, and the aesthetic look you're going for, given that different glazes create very different appearances on your pottery. Let's take a closer look at the different things you'll want to consider before making a choice of glaze that will work for you.

Firing Temperature

The temperature at which you're firing your ceramic vessel is important since glazes need to reach a particular temperature in order to melt and bond with your ceramic properly. Some glazes work best in higher temperatures. On the other hand, some are better suited for mid or low temperatures.

As you already know, temperature ranges for your kiln are called cones. The name comes from small pieces of cone-shaped ceramics placed in kilns. Each cone has a different melting point, and they are given numbers that correspond to the temperatures at which they bend and finally collapse.

The lowest cone, as mentioned previously, is 022, and ceramics of this cone melt at approximately 1,112 degrees Fahrenheit (600 degrees Celsius). The highest cone is 10, and ceramics of this cone melt at approximately 23,82 degrees Fahrenheit (1,305 degrees Celsius). There are higher cones, but for most commercial purposes, 10 is the highest.

While these cones pertain to the temperatures at which different clays melt, glazes are also categorized according to this cone system. When you're choosing a glaze, it's important to select one that should be fired at the same temperature as the clay body. So, with that said, let's look at the general firing ranges of glazes.

- **Low-Fire Glazes**: These are for glazes that have firing ranges of temperatures between 1,830 to 1,940 degrees Fahrenheit (999 - 1,060 degrees Celsius). This generally means they correspond to cones 06 through 04. These glazes are capable of producing strong colors, but without the need for as much power. This makes them a more economical option. There are many glazes available in this firing range.

- **Mid-Fire Glazes**: These require temperatures ranging between 2,157 to 2,232 degrees Fahrenheit (1,186 to 1,222 degrees Fahrenheit) for firing. Generally speaking, this means cones 4 through 6. Traditionally, the medium and high-fire glazes have been used for pottery that has more earthy, subdued colors, but glazes have made some great advances in recent years. Nowadays, it is possible to achieve vivid colors with glazes that require firing in this temperature range. A major advantage of these kinds of glazes is that they're usually strong, which makes them great for functional purposes. There are many glazes available in this firing range.

- **High-Fire Glazes**: Glazes in this category are fired at temperatures between 2,305 and 2,381 degrees Fahrenheit (1,263 and 1,305 degrees Celsius). This typically means cones 8 through 10. Most electric kilns aren't able to fire at this high temperature range in part because it draws so much electricity. For that reason, if you need to fire ceramics in this range, it's likely you'll need to acquire a gas kiln. Gas kilns aren't used as much as electric ones, and that's why there are fewer commercially produced glazes that require these temperature ranges available. All the same, you can find recipes for glazes in high-fire ranges by going into online forums. Potters are, as a rule, generous in sharing their recipes.

You do have to be careful about over or under-firing your glaze. If you don't fire the glaze at an appropriate temperature, it will cause problems. Over-firing, for instance, can cause the clay to melt and slide down the pottery, which results in an accumulation of glaze at the bottom of your ceramic piece. What's left on the rest of the vessel will then be relatively thin. You can also get blistering, which is exactly what it sounds like, and pinholing, which results in small holes all over the surface of the glaze. The holes are caused when bubbles burst in the glaze as it is turning red. They go all the way down to the surface of the clay that underlies the glaze. Pitting is a defect that is similar to pinholing, but the holes are more shallow and don't reach the clay surface. These problems are why it is important to avoid over-firing your glaze.

At the opposite extreme, under-firing your glaze also causes problems. Under-firing results in glaze that has not been heated sufficiently, and it can result in a cloudy, dull, or matte appearance to the ceramic. It can also cause a rougher texture, much like a piece of glass that gets washed up on the beach. The problem here is that the melting process was interrupted so that the glaze was unable to fully 'mature.' It is possible to re-fire the glaze if this happens, but only if the underlying clay can withstand that as well. This is why the glaze and the clay both should be a match for firing temperature. You can find out what the firing temperature for the clay is in most cases by looking at the bag, and you should be sure to choose a pottery glaze that matches that.

It's important to match them both because the glaze interacts with the underlying clay as it melts. In fact, the glaze and the clay interact to form an intermediate layer between both, and the more they mix in this layer, the stronger the bond will be. Bonding is what happens when both the glaze and the clay reach their peaks at the same time in the firing process.

Type of Kiln

Another consideration when choosing your glaze is the type of kiln you're using. There are two general types: electric and gas. There are other ways to fire pottery, but, particularly if you're new to this, you'll likely be using a gas or electric kiln. Electric kilns are a lot more common than gas, partly because of the convenience factor. Gas kilns need an air inlet and a flue to vent the gas. Electric kilns do not need any venting. That makes electric kilns cheaper to buy. You might, however, be able to rent or borrow a gas kiln for firing even if you buy an electric one.

Oxidation and Reduction: The kiln you're using is an important consideration. Glazes look different when they are fired in an electric kiln versus a gas kiln. Oxidation and reduction are the chemical processes that happen during firing, and the processes differ depending on how much oxygen is present in the kiln's atmosphere.

Typically, a reduction atmosphere is created in a gas kiln, but not in an electric kiln. Electric kilns create an oxidation atmosphere.

When a ceramic glaze is fired in an oxidation atmosphere - as is created in an electric kiln - it tends to result in clean, bright colors. The same glaze fired in the reduction atmosphere created in a gas kiln will look more earthy and organic. Reduction atmospheres result in more intense and darker glazes. This might seem perhaps overly technical to you, but it's something you have to consider as you're choosing a glaze.

Decorative or Functional Glazes

What you're going to be using the glaze for is another significant consideration. Will the vessel be used for decorative or functional purposes? If you're going to be eating off the vessel, you definitely need to give some careful thought to what's on its surface. That way, you can choose something that will hold up if you're cooking on it. You also can ensure the surface is non-toxic if you're planning to eat food from it.

If your pottery is solely for decorative purposes, like a vase, then you have more options available to you, but if it's something you'll be eating off of, it obviously needs to be food-safe. This is something that has come under increasing scrutiny, and it's actually quite complex. Matte or non-glossy glazes are frequently not safe for food because they can harbor bacteria. Crackle glazes that have tiny cracks on the surface have the same problem. These types of glazes have the potential as well to leach toxic substances into the food. A substance of particular concern is lead.

Lead can make the surface of your vessel glossy and bright, but you certainly do not want to consume it. It is not only toxic, but it also accumulates over time in your system, and it stays in your system. So, if you somehow consumed lead as a child, that is still present in your system, and you'll be adding to that if you're eating off or drinking out of ceramic vessels that have a lead glaze on them. Lead also poses a health hazard to the potter, so if you are using a glaze that contains lead, you'll need to be overly strict about your safety procedures. Almost all, if not all, glaze suppliers will clearly state whether or not their product contains lead.

While lead is a major concern, it is not the only chemical that can cause problems for utilitarian pottery. Pottery must be fired to maturity as well as be lead-free to be considered food-safe. It also has to have a suitable clay body. Because that isn't certain, many suppliers will not certify that a glaze is food-safe unless it has been tested in a laboratory. There are laboratories that are certified for testing ceramics, and they can test your pottery for any leaching of toxic substances. While that sounds tedious, it's actually a pretty easy process. You just send them a sample, and you'll get an answer quite quickly.

Of course, if you're making a functional vessel, you'll want to choose a lead-free glaze, but, to be sure it's safe from other possible toxic substances, it's worthwhile to get it tested. Ask yourself if you would want it tested before you allow your family to eat from it, and then proceed as appropriate. It's almost a must to test them if you're selling them, but on the bright side, it gives you something to advertise.

Artistic Considerations

Another consideration is the artistry of the object. While it's not a practical health concern like the above-mentioned considerations, it's still very important. It all depends on the look you're going for. A clear glaze that's applied directly to the bisque clay body, for example, yields a clean piece of ceramic. This might be the better choice if you want to emphasize the form of the vessel rather than something like color. It's also a good choice if you've applied an underglaze decoration. The glaze applied over that will seal the ceramic so that it's non-porous.

Colors from underglazes can be very vivid. If fired correctly, the colors will survive the process and stay true to the original appearance. In fact, a clear glaze applied over the top of colorful underglaze decorations will intensify those colors even more. You can also use a translucent glaze to cover the underglaze, but most potters choose a clear glaze instead. Among the clear glazes, you can choose from glossy, matte, or satin/semi-matte.

You do have to be careful to avoid smudging the underglaze when you're applying the clear glaze. You can avoid this using one of several techniques. You might, for example, spray the underglaze with hair spray or liquid laundry starch to fix it. That can stop it from running when you apply the clear glaze, and either of those substances will burn off when fired in the kiln. You can also avoid smudging by taking care when you apply the glaze. Using a thin, light layer first can minimize smudging if you allow that to dry before building up the layers. Alternatively, you can also dip your glaze on rather than brushing, and that will help avoid smudging.

Method of Application

Another consideration is the method you'll be using to apply the glaze. Two of the most common methods used are dipping or brushing.

Dipping Glazes: Dipping your vessel in a glaze means you're submerging it completely. Typically, you'll hold it in the glaze for around three seconds and then remove it. This allows you to coat the pottery quickly, and it's the method preferred if you're producing larger quantities of pottery. This involves using a larger quantity of glaze, however, and that's one downside to the method. Most ready-made dipping glazes are sold by the gallon, so you'll have a large container into which you can dip your pieces. If you're just working with a few pieces or even one piece, this is not necessarily an economical or practical method to use.

Brushing Glazes: Brushing glazes, unlike dipping glazes, are sold in smaller quantities. They also are usually thicker in consistency since most brush glazes are formulated to ensure that the brush marks will even out after the glaze is applied. This doesn't always work, though, so you want to be careful to apply it as evenly as possible unless you want the brush marks to be part of your decoration.

A Mix: There are some glazes that make the claim they are suitable for either dipping or brushing. If you're dipping, you'll only need to apply one coat. If you're brushing the glaze on, then you'll likely need to apply at least two or three coats. These mixed-purpose glazes are usually thicker than glazes that are marketed as dipping glazes. You can thin the glaze out, however, by adding water until it reaches the desired consistency.

Powdered or Ready-Made

Another consideration is how the glaze comes. If it comes as a ready-made glaze, it should be in liquid form, and if it's a powder, you'll need to mix it with water before you can use it. Powdered glazes are less expensive, but ready-made glazes are more convenient. If you're new to this, you might want to choose the ready-made glaze; it's one less thing you'll have to worry about. Using a ready-made glaze means it will be the correct thickness and consistency. Once you feel confident that you're familiar with the correct consistency, you can experiment with mixing the glaze yourself.

Most glazes that come in powdered form also come with instructions for mixing them. This will involve adding a certain amount of water to get the correct ratio, but once it's mixed, you'll also want to pass it through a sieve. This is so that you can smooth out any lumps that might be in the mixture. Some glazes, however, are designed to produce a speckled effect, and, if that is the case, you'll want to return the material in the sieve to the mixture. You want that gritty residue for creating the speckled effect.

If you're mixing your own glaze, you can choose between a dipping or brushing glaze. If you want to brush it on, you'll simply add a thickening agent. Each glaze supplier will have their own brand of thickener, and they will typically advise you on what ratio of glaze to thickener you should use for brushing on the glaze.

Colored Glazes

There are many different colored glazes to choose from; it's really a matter of your choice regarding what you like in a color scheme. Usually, you want to apply layers of different colored glazes on the same piece of ceramic. Layering can really create a number of beautiful, unique results. You need to be careful, though, about what temperatures each mature at. You don't want to layer a low-fire glaze with a high-fire glaze since that will likely look odd. Either glaze will suffer from the firing process, depending on which temperature you go for. Maybe you want to create an odd-looking glaze, so if that's your goal, then this is one way to accomplish that.

It's important to remember that raw glazes in an unfired state will look very different from those that have been fired. The opacity of your glaze will also be affected by the color of your clay. You might notice that your ceramic comes out looking very different from the sample piece that the supplier used for illustration purposes. Depending on whether you like the results or not, that might be exciting or disappointing. Maybe the key is to keep an open mind about the results. Let yourself be flexible about the results you are trying to achieve. You might really love the result even though it isn't necessarily what you intended.

Types of Glaze

There are several different types of glazes to consider. Let's look at what each does and the benefits and drawbacks of each.

Transparent glazes: If you prefer a transparent glaze, you'll see any underglaze decoration as well as the clay body through the glaze. You also should remember that transparent glaze darkens and/or intensifies the color of any underglaze and the clay body itself. For that reason, a transparent glaze can sometimes compromise the color you had in mind for the underglaze design. If you combine the two wisely, however, the combination can work well.

Opaque glazes: In contrast to transparent glazes, opaque glazes will block out the color of the clay body. You'll want to use these in the cases where you'd like the glaze to serve as the main decoration. You can, however, get a semi-transparent glaze that will only partially block out the underlying clay body or underglaze.

Breaking glazes: These kinds of glazes are specifically formulated so that they will become thinner over any raised areas on the ceramic piece. That way, they serve to highlight the various textures on the surface of the piece. These can, for instance, bring out incised patterns on the clay surface or raised contours. They do this because they become thinner on raised surfaces and then pool in recessed areas of the vessel. If the body of your vessel is a different color from the glaze, any incised designs can be highlighted more clearly with a breaking glaze. You might, as an example, use a dark glaze on a light-colored clay to really highlight the incised patterns.

Flowing glazes: As the name suggests, these glazes become very fluid and move around when they are fired. These are frequently applied in combination with other glazes, and they are typically used on top or below the other glaze. They bleed when they are fired, and that moves them into the glazes next to them. These glazes are most frequently fired at lower temperatures, most often between cones 06 to 05. If they are fired at higher temperatures, though, they can produce similar effects to those glazes that are typically fired at those temperatures. It's a great way for potters to recreate a higher fired glaze appearance at lower temperatures.

If you want to control how the flowing glaze turns out, you'll want to apply it to particular patterns. That will give you some control, but each piece will look different when finished because of the movement during firing. Those types of glazes that move less are described as 'stiffer.' By choosing a stiffer glaze, you can exercise more control over the final result.

Textured glazes: Glazes most often come in gloss, matte, semi-matte, semi-gloss, and satin matte, but there are some that are manufactured specifically to have a textured finish. A common one is called 'crackle glaze.' These are designed to produce a crazed kind of effect once they are fired. This can be faint and only visible on close inspection or it can be distinctive and bold. Other effects include pitted, cobbled, frothy, or mottled, and you can choose any of these kinds of textured finishes.

You can also use the application technique you choose to create glaze textures. You can use different kinds of tools to texture the glaze in a similar manner to what you might do when painting something like a wall.

Raku glazes: Raku refers to a particular way to fire your pottery. With Raku, you take the pottery out using tongs when it is red hot. You then put the piece into a combustible material and cover it so that you create a reduction atmosphere. The sudden drop in temperature causes the glaze to crack, and the carbon that results from the combustible material gets embedded into the cracks in the glaze. This results in a dark-colored crazed pattern that can be set against a lighter-colored glaze. It's a very distinctive Raku appearance.

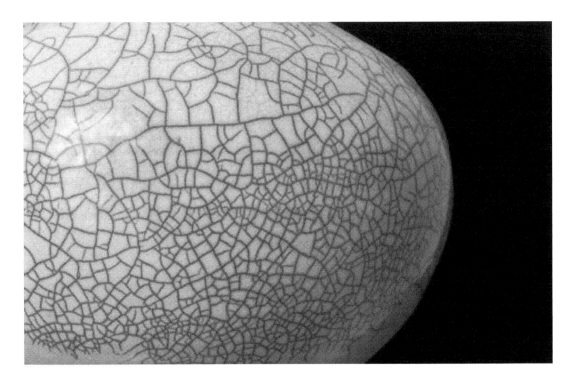

Technically speaking, any glaze that is used with this Raku firing technique is considered a Raku glaze, but there are some kinds of glazes that are designed to enhance the Raku effect when they are fired. These include glazes that have metallic lusters and crackled patterns.

While the Raku technique involves a reduction atmosphere, this can also be created in an oxidation atmosphere. It does present a different result, though, since a reduction atmosphere is created when the ceramics are sealed in with a combustible material. These ceramics will typically display earthier colors, metallic tones, and a speckling or crackle effect.

Luster overglaze: These kinds of glazes have metallic and iridescent effects on ceramics that are already glazed and have been fired. This kind of glaze is applied over a glazed surface, and the ceramic vessel is fired anew at a low temperature. Typically, these are re-fired at between cone 018 and cone 016. That will prevent the softening of the existing glaze on the piece. If that underlying glaze does start to melt again, the look of the luster glaze will be compromised.

Luster glazes are usually composed of ingredients that melt at lower temperatures. Just like any other glaze, they can be applied by dipping them, painting them on, or by spraying them on. You can also use a luster pen to draw the glaze on your previously glazed ceramic piece. Luster glazes are nice if you want to add some pizzazz to your pieces.

In sum, there are several considerations when choosing a glaze to use on your pottery. The choice is dependent on several factors, including practical, technical, and artistic considerations. Glazing simply involves an element of surprise. While you can exercise a certain amount of control, there are so many factors in play that you can never be certain of the exact outcome. You'll just have to wait until your piece emerges from the kiln to see what you've got. That's why it's a good idea to embrace the unexpected. Let yourself be surprised and learn to experiment with different outcomes. You might end up with something much more beautiful than you had expected or intended.

Chapter Summary

In this chapter, we've explored the various glazes and the different considerations when choosing the one you will use. Specifically, we've covered the following topics:

- How the firing temperature affects the choice of glaze;

- How the different kilns affect your glaze options;

- How the use of the ceramic piece affects your choice;

- What the method of application has to do with your choice;

- The different types of glazes available.

In the next chapter, you will learn about the brushing method of glaze application.

Chapter Five: Brushing Your Glazes

As we have seen, glazing is a necessary part of making pottery because it conveys many advantages to the ceramic vessel. There are several different ways you can apply a glaze to your pottery, and which one you choose depends on the effect you're trying to create.

Brushing on the glaze is one application method that uses a brush to apply the glaze. It results in a number of different design possibilities that include multiple layers, gives you a lot of versatility, and allows you to express your creativity. This method, though, requires that you pay attention to the details, and it will likely take some practice too.

As a beginner potter, you might find it challenging to create an even surface using this technique, and if you don't have any intricate design details, you might want to consider dipping the piece instead of brushing. But, this technique does allow you to do a variety of designs not possible with other methods of glaze application. Let's explore the advantages and disadvantages of this method in more depth.

Advantages of Brushing on Glaze

While this is one technique that takes time to perfect, it has a number of benefits, particularly if you're working on a unique piece. The following are advantages of using this technique over others:

- You'll be able to use the broadest range of both colors and visual effects. While the technique requires exceptional control, it also allows you to create intricate design elements that simply aren't possible with dipping, bubbling, or even sponging.

- You can create more depth with your ceramic vessels because the different types of brushes give you more freedom to apply composite layers.

- You really can't do this method incorrectly, particularly since you can create multiple layers, which will allow you to cover any imperfections in your designs.

- It's a less expensive method because, with something like dipping, you'll end up making several different buckets of glaze to create multiple layers on the ceramic vessel. With brushing, you'll only use enough glaze to cover the vessel, so you won't be mixing up anything extra.

- Brush glazing uses a thicker glaze, and that means that you won't see or create as many imperfections as you do with other methods of application.

- Different types of brushes that you use with this method will allow you to create some very intricate special effects on a ceramic vessel. You can layer the glaze, use metallic glaze, or create bright colors for your pottery.

- These advantages make brushing on your glaze a favored application technique among potters, but it does require practice. There are also a few disadvantages that you should consider before deciding on this technique.

Disadvantages of Brushing on Glaze

While brushing on the glaze gives you complete control over the design elements you create on a vessel, some potters still don't like to use this technique. These are some of the most common reasons they cite.

- This technique does require that you use a combination of commercially prepared glazes and your own recipes. With dip glazing, you can use your own powder glaze, but you really have to use prepared glazes with brushing, and that means it can cost more, particularly if you're glazing several ceramics.

- Prepared glazes don't list what's in the glaze. If you're using a powder to create your glaze, you'll know exactly what's in it, but with prepared glazes, you may not, and that can result in some adverse effects.

- This type of glazing is slower than other methods. It takes longer for brushed-on glazes to dry, and you're going to need a minimum of three coats. That means you'll have to let each coat dry before going on to the next one. If you're doing more layers than simply three, it can become quite time intensive.

- Now that you have a better idea of the advantages and disadvantages of this technique, let's talk about the basics for beginners.

Basics of Brushing on Glaze

Beginners often prefer this technique because of the advantages it gives them. You have that full control over your designs, of course, but the technique is not as simple as it might seem. You need to take some very specific steps if you're going to be successful using this approach. These are the basics you'll need to know before you start brushing.

Preparation for Glazing

While it is possible to use the brushing technique to apply glaze to what is called greenware--that's the bone-dry stage of clay where it's been shaped and dried but not fired--it's not recommended for a few reasons. First, the more you handle greenware, the more likely you are to break or crack the piece. Second, firing your greenware before glazing helps to prevent it from cracking, crazing, or flaking because it releases the organic gases from the clay.

That's why, in preparation for glazing, it's recommended that you fire the bisque ware to at least 1,828 degrees Fahrenheit (1,000 degrees Celsius), which is cone 06. That creates the best surface for applying a glaze. After you've fired it, remove any dust from the surface with a damp sponge, and if you're working on a piece that has a narrow neck, you'll also want to use a moist brush to wipe out the interior. You also want to make sure the surface is free from any grease. If glaze is applied to a greasy surface, it can crawl or fail to adhere properly to the piece when it's fired.

After you've properly fired and cleaned the vessel, you should choose the brush that's right for what you want to do. You want to minimize the streaking that will inevitably occur. There are a number of specialized brushes, like Hake or Soft Fan, that will help keep the streaking to a minimum. You should go for a brush that will let you load up a decent amount of glaze, and you'll also want the right brushes to work with various colors. If you have multiple sizes of pieces, you'll want to get a set of glaze brushes that can help to minimize unevenness, but still allow for versatility in creating the designs you want.

Mixing the Glaze

Once your piece is ready and you've chosen your brushes, the next step is to mix the glaze. It's important to mix it well and strain it so that it can be properly applied to the ceramic. You want it to turn out right after all the work you've done up to this point. Undoubtedly, you'll have the experience of waiting anxiously for the kiln to cool so you can see what you've created only to find that it didn't turn out at all. By preparing the glaze appropriately, you can reduce the number of times that happens.

By mixing your glaze thoroughly and then straining to remove any clumps or debris, you stand a better chance of getting the result you're hoping to achieve. Even with bottle glazes, you should still mix them before brushing them on your piece. You want a nice, even consistency, but remember that glaze dries fast, so you'll need to be prepared to keep going once you've started mixing the glaze. You can add water, but you should only do so if the glaze is thicker than what you want for the piece you're working on.

It's really a good idea to work with glazes that are designed for brushing since it is difficult to add in the thickening and stabilizing agents necessary to something like a dipping glaze to make it suitable for brushing. That's really not the best option for beginners, so it's better to either use prepared glazes designed for brushing or mix a brushing powder glaze specific to that purpose. When your glaze has been thoroughly mixed and sieved, it's ready to be applied.

Glaze Application

Brushing glazes are typically stored in either pint or gallon bottles, so that's what you'll want to use to be sure you have enough glaze on hand. You'll need to apply glaze layers to a sufficiently thick level so that you don't end up with unwanted streaking. Start by loading up your brush to the degree that your glaze, in effect, floats onto the pottery. Change the direction of your brush strokes with each coat you apply. If your first coat is diagonal, the second could be vertical, and the third horizontal. The direction doesn't matter, but vary it with each coat. That will even out the thickness and reduce streak marks. You continue brushing on the glaze for at least three layers and perhaps more if that's what your design calls for.

Another method of applying brushed glaze is to use a pottery wheel or banding wheel. With this technique, you simply place the piece on the wheel, load your brush, and spin the pottery while applying the glaze with your brush. With either application technique, you can really let your imagination go wild in creating various designs. You might make different colored bands, for example, or float some indiscriminate heavy coats on different parts of the vessel. There are a number of different possibilities. You might even want to create streaking on purpose. If you're going for a smooth finish, load the brush, apply three flowing coats of the glaze, and allow each to dry in between coats. There are all sorts of possibilities with this method of application so let the creativity flow.

In sum, though brush glazing is more time-consuming than some of the other methods, it offers more intricate design opportunities. It's also possible to use a combination of application techniques, like dipping and brushing, for example, to achieve the best finish for your vessels. The possibilities really are endless. It's just a matter of practicing each and deciding what works best for you and the piece you're making.

Chapter Summary

In this chapter, we've discussed the brushing method of applying glaze. Specifically, we've talked about the following topics:

- The advantages and disadvantages of brushing on glaze;

- The basics of brush glazing;

- Glazing preparation;

- Glaze mixing;

- Glaze application.

In the next chapter, you will learn about the dipping method of applying glaze.

Chapter Six: Dipping Your Glazes

Dipping glaze is another way to apply glaze to your ceramic vessel. There are two main uses of dipping glazes in traditional ceramics: 1) For the application of a single layer, and; 2) for the application of layers on top of a glaze layer. Let's examine the advantages and disadvantages of dipping, and then we'll discuss the application uses and techniques.

Advantages of Dipping

1. Dipping your ceramic is a very fast method for applying glaze;

2. Dipping is a good method for getting an even coat to the glaze;

3. If you dip with care, you can use different glazes for the inside and the outside.

Disadvantages of Dipping

1. It can't be used with heavy ceramics because their weight can cause an upward thrust while dipping. That might cause the glaze to pour off of the container.
2. It's not the best technique for multiple glazing.

Single Layer Base-Coat Application

If you're planning on creating a single layer base-coat application of glaze on a ceramic vessel, dipping is the method you want to use. It dries quickly and you get an even coverage if your glaze mixture is done correctly. To make your mixture just right, you want to create a thixotropic suspension. This kind of suspension will flow when you need it to flow, and then it will gel after just a few moments of sitting. That will give you a drip-free coverage.

Some glazes will behave like motor oil where they will continuously drip, but thixotropic glazes--also called engobes--don't do that. Instead, they go on evenly with good thickness, and they don't run or drip. To get a thixotropic solution, you need to add sufficient water and a flocculant like vinegar, Epsom salts, or calcium chloride. That will give you a creamy glaze slurry that is also thixotropic. This is where measuring the specific gravity of the glaze is helpful.

Specific gravity is also known as relative density because you're measuring the ratio of the density of one substance, in this case your glaze slurry, to a standard substance, usually water. In other words, you're determining the ratio of water in the slurry to solid materials. The slurry you apply to the body of a ceramic vessel needs to have a controlled specific gravity for good performance.

Water has a specific gravity of 1.0, and if your slurry has a specific gravity of 1.8, that means it is 1.8 times heavier than water. There are a number of ways to determine specific gravity, but one basic way is to simply weigh a container and record its weight. Then, weigh it full of water and record that measurement. Finally, weigh it full of your glaze slurry and record that measurement. The amount of water and glaze slurry you're weighing should be the same. Now subtract the weight of the container from both measurements. You're left with the weight of the water and the weight of the slurry. Divide the weight of your slurry with the weight of the water, and you'll have the specific gravity of the slurry. You'll know how much heavier it is than water.

While casting slips have a specific desirable range for specific gravity, glazes are different. It depends on your process. You might have a glaze that approaches the same specific gravity desired for slips--1.75--but most potters like to have their glazes somewhere between 1.45 and 1.50. To get a thixotropic property in your dipping glaze, you will require a lower specific gravity--between 1.43 and 1.45--and you'll add the flocculant. This compares to most brushing glazes that will have a specific gravity of 1.55 and most clear glazes which are brushed on in a very thin layer that have a specific gravity of 1.25.

The thixotropic property in your glaze will reduce the viscosity as the slurry is moving, but then that viscous state will recover when the movement stops. That means your glaze will gel after it stops moving, and that will keep it from dripping. Some of the more common fluids you will very likely have had personal experience of, and which are highly thixotropic, include your toothpaste, mayonnaise, ketchup, hair gel, and the like.

For a single layer base-coat application to your vessel, you want to at least dip the inside functional surfaces, but the method works even better if you also want to cover large outer areas with dipping. The thixotropic glaze will harden because of the clay in the recipe, and, therefore, it's easy to make and fast to apply. Moreover, the materials you need to make a glaze thixotropic are all common and readily available.

Multiple Layer Application

If you're applying multiple layers to the vessel, your glaze will need to contain a binder, typically gum, to get it to fix to the body of the vessel and harden as it dries. For a binder to be effective, you require a glaze that contains super-fine particles that the binder can bind with, and these kinds of glazes tend to dry slower as well as drip while draining. The individual layers will be thinner as well. Unless you're serious about developing your own recipes for making gummed glazes, most potters will simply purchase commercially bottled and gummed products for this purpose.

Thixotropic Glaze Recipe for Dipping

To make a thixotropic glaze, you'll want to make sure you're wearing a mask. Sprinkle the glaze powder into your container of water and stir it thoroughly. Let it settle overnight and then you can pour off the excess water. Stir the mixture again and sieve it through a #80 mesh, or finer, sieve. Add any water you need to get the consistency you want. While the consistency depends on the porosity of your bisque ware, you will typically have a mixture of approximately 880 to 1230 grams of powder to 1,000 milliliters of water. Some glazes require less water; it just depends on what you're glazing.

You'll want to add a flocculant to the mixture to keep the glaze from setting. Epsom salts are commonly used for this. Add the flocculant and stir until you see that the settling stops. Don't add too much or it will cause the glaze to dry too slowly on the vessel itself. That can result in 'mud cracking' or crawling during firing. If you add too much, there is a solution. Simply add small quantities of a 10 percent solution of deflocculant. Soda ash, Dispex, or sodium silicate are examples, and you can stir them into the mixture until you see the optimal consistency and good drying.

Applying a Dipping Glaze

Dipping is one of the easiest methods for the application of glazes, but there are several different ways to dip. The following are not an exhaustive list, and, as the last method implies, you might even improvise to come up with a better way.

It's always a good idea after you've prepared your dipping glaze to apply it to a few sample pieces so that you can evaluate your mixture. That way, you can make any adjustments to the consistency before applying it to the pieces you're working on. Once you have the mixture you want, here are a few techniques to use for various types of ceramics.

Mugs and Bowls: For mugs and bowls, you'll require the tongs to be located near the top weld of the handle. That way, you won't end up with easily visible tong marks after you've fired it. It's also helpful to put the vertical tines of the tong on the outside of the piece to minimize the visibility of the marks. When you're ready, do the following:

- Dip the mug into your glaze slurry at an angle, a bit like using it as a ladle. You don't want to pour straight down into the mixture since that can cause it to splash back up at you. It can get messy that way, and it could get in your eyes, too.

- Hold the piece in the slurry mixture for between two and five seconds, depending on the glaze setup.

- Remove the piece from the glaze by angling it back out in reverse of what you did in the first step. You're trying to keep any splashing to a minimum.

- Hold your tongs in an upright position so that the piece is upside down and right above the glaze bucket.

- Twist the tongs around in a circular motion to keep the wet glaze on the rim of the vessel from gathering in one spot. Gently shake the piece to cause the excess glaze to run off and the coating to smooth out.

- Once the rim no longer has a wet sheen, you can set the piece down in its upright position.

- Now you can inspect your ceramic. Is the coat smooth? Are there areas of dripping that could show up on the fired piece? If so, that can indicate that you don't have your glaze correctly set up or that you set the piece down before it was really dry enough.

Flat Items (like Plates) Using Tongs: For this type of application, you can do the following:

- Gently slide the plate or other type of flatware into the glaze mixture rim first so that it won't cause splashing.

- Hold the item in the glaze for between two and five seconds.

- Remove the flatware while holding it vertically, and then shake off any extra glaze.

- Set it down after it has lost that wet sheen appearance.

- To remove the tong marks, you can smooth that area with a brush or Q-tip.

- **Glazing Tall, Narrow Cylinders, and Vases**: This technique is for those kinds of items that are tall and narrow:

- Hold the ceramic vase by its bottom and dip it rim-first into your glaze mixture one-third to one-half of the vessel's height.

- In one quick motion, push the vase straight down into the mixture. Then, snap it up, but not out of the glaze. You'll hear a burping sound which is caused as the interior is glazed.

- Remove the piece and let it dry until you no longer see that wet sheen. Check inside to ensure the interior has been adequately covered with glaze.

- Turn the piece over while holding the neck area with tongs, and now, plunge it bottom first into the glaze mixture. You want to dip it to the point where there is a slight overlap with the area you glazed in the first step of the procedure. After thls, remove the ceramic, and set it down so it can dry.

Car Dent Remover Technique for Several Types of Vessels: This is a great, innovative technique for dipping glaze without using tongs or your fingers. It's particularly useful for pieces that are too wide or awkward to grip with the tongs safely. It can also be used on those pieces where you really don't want to have tong or finger marks.

You might have seen commercials for those car dent removers that will allow you to suction out small dents from a car's body. Well, they can also work very nicely for dipping ceramics. They have a comfortable handle you can hold on to, and that is attached to a powerful suction cup. The smallest available car dent remover is 2.5 inches (6 centimeters) in diameter, and they can hold a ceramic that weighs up to 11 pounds (5 kilograms). You just have to make sure that the seal of the suction cup is good. Then, do the following:

- Apply wax resist to a small area of the vessel that is a little bigger than the dent remover diameter. That will help it create a good seal. You can also add a little water to the suction cup.

- Position the dent remover centrally on your piece and press down firmly as you move the lever to the 'attach' setting.

- Check to ensure your piece is firmly attached, then dip as you would normally with tongs.

- When the piece is dry enough to handle it without disturbing the glaze, you can remove the dent remover.

- Dipping is one of the easier ways to apply ceramic glaze, and you can even get innovative with different techniques for holding onto the ceramic piece. The key to successful dipping is the consistency of your glaze and its ability to set up quickly after you've dipped your vessel. It's a great technique for achieving a smooth finish on your work.

Chapter Summary

In this chapter, we've covered the dipping technique of applying glaze to vessels. Specifically, we've covered the following topics;

- The advantages and disadvantages of the dipping technique;

- Two uses of dipping glazes;

- Applying a single layer;

- Applying multiple layers;

- The importance of thixotropic properties;

- A dipping glaze recipe;

- Several dipping glaze techniques for different kinds of vessels.

In the next chapter, you will learn all about pouring glazes.

Chapter Seven: Pouring Your Glazes

Pouring your glaze is another fine method you can use to apply glaze to your ceramics. The advantages of this technique include that it's another fast way to apply the glaze. It's also particularly advantageous for certain shapes of ceramics. Bowls, the outside of vases, and some flatware are examples of the shapes for which it is easier to pour a glaze than using other techniques. It's also a helpful technique for applying cover glazes like flat colors, transparent glazes, or white glazes. That being said, one of the main disadvantages is that it can be more difficult to control the flow of your glaze than with other methods.

The consistency of your glaze should be similar to that for dipping glazes and for the same reasons. You want it to flow while you're pouring, but set up and not drip when the vessel is drying. For that, you need the thixotropic properties that we've looked at in the previous chapter. Just as with the dipping glazes, you'll want to ensure you have a good specific gravity; usually 1.5 to 1.6 is a good thickness for pouring glaze. It's a little thinner than the dipping glaze, which works well for pouring.

The Technique for Pouring Glaze

A great tool to use for pouring glaze is simple to find in most gardening shops. It's a watering can with a spout that pours from the bottom of the can. It ensures a strong, constant stream of glaze and it also reduces bubbles. Once you have the tools you need, following these steps:

Step 1: Glaze the Inside of the Vessel

- Fill your watering can with your glaze mixture.

- Begin by pouring the inside of the vessel. After you've glazed an area, you don't want to handle it too much. If you started with the outside of the vessel, then you would have a greater chance of leaving marks or messing up the outside glaze as you move on to the inside.

- To glaze the inside of your ceramic, hold it over a basin and simply pour the mixture into the pot and leave it for three seconds. Then, quickly pour it back into the glaze bucket. You can flick off any excess by sharply rotating your wrist while you keep the pot's rim parallel to the floor. You can also wipe it off with a towel or a sponge, or you could choose to leave it for decorative effect.

- It helps to keep rotating the piece as you continuously pour the glaze, and you might also need to rotate it back and forth two or three times so as to get an even coverage.

- While pouring the inside, you might end up with small holes where the glaze has not covered the clay. You can use a small brush with some watered-down glaze to fill those holes. Be sure that the substance is watery enough to be absorbed into the hole.

- While pouring the inside of your vessel, it's inevitable that some glaze will end up on the outside of the piece. To remove it, scrape it with a blade of some kind. After that, you can sponge off any glaze that still remains on the exterior.

- Once you've finished with the inside, you want to wait until the next day to glaze the outside. That way, you won't overload your bisque ware with water.

Step 2: Glaze the Outside of the Piece

- When you're ready to pour the outside of the vessel, you can do a few things depending on the size and shape of the vessel. For vessels that have an interior glaze, you can protect that by placing a plaster model with a soft piece of sponge over the top of it in the opening. That should protect the inner surface.

- For a bowl: put a basin on top of your banding wheel and make a bridge across it with two pieces of wood. Then, turn your bowl upside down and place it on the bridge. Pour the liquid over it, starting at the top and letting the glaze run down. While you're doing this, turn the banding wheel until you've covered the entire vessel. Be sure to rotate the wheel at sufficient speed so that the glaze can't gather on the inside rim of the vessel. Quick note - if your bowl curves inward, this is not the best technique to use. Dipping is better in that case.

- For flatware: hold the plate with the right side up over a bucket where you're keeping your glaze supply. Pour your glaze over the center of the flatware--about two to three spoonful's worth of glaze--and then tilt the plate until the liquid covers it completely. Move it around several times, and then tilt the unnecessary glaze back into the bucket and clean the edge. After that dries, you can do the other side.

- Be careful not to overlap the inside and outside glazes, but, if that does happen, you can let everything dry, then use fine sandpaper to gently remove extra glaze so that you have an even application over the entire vessel.

- The properties of your glaze are what will determine how long you should pour it. For a glaze with a specific gravity of 1.48, you typically want to pour for four to five seconds while turning the wheel to keep it from running into the foot of the ceramic.

- If you do get excess glaze on the rim or foot, you can scrape it off using a rib after it has dried. Then, you can use a wet, clean sponge to clean it.

Pouring glaze is another fast, relatively easy way to apply glaze to ceramics. It has distinct advantages for certain types of vessels, but it's not a suitable method for intricate work as it's more difficult to control the flow of the glaze. All the same, it's a great method for beginners to master.

Chapter Summary

In this chapter, we've discussed the pouring method of glaze application. Specifically, we've covered the following topics:

- The advantages and disadvantages of pouring glaze;

- The technique for pouring glaze;

- Pouring the inside of the vessel;

- Pouring the outside of the vessel.

In the next chapter, you will learn about the spraying technique for applying glaze.

Chapter Eight: Spraying Your Glazes

Another great technique for applying glaze to ceramic vessels is to spray it on. That requires some special equipment like spray guns or airbrushes. You'll also need a compressed air stream that will move the glazing materials through the gun and its atomizing nozzle. The spray gun or airbrush acts as a pneumatic sprayer in this way.

To spray glaze, you will have to make sure you have nozzles large enough to allow the glaze particles to pass through without becoming plugged up. This technique will also require a spray booth that has good ventilation so that you won't make a mess of your work area. You'll also need to make sure you're taking the appropriate safety precautions that include wearing a respirator so that you're not inhaling the aerosolized glaze. Let's begin by examining the advantages and disadvantages of this method.

Advantages of Spraying on Glaze

1. Spraying is a very useful approach if you are glazing a large quantity of pottery with the same glaze. You can just mix up a bucket and start spraying.
2. This method also allows you to make subtle color variations as compared to dipping or pouring.
3. This method also gives you more control over the glaze coverage and thickness.

Disadvantages of Spraying on Glaze

1. You need a larger quantity of glazing material since you need to ensure sufficient thickness to cover your pieces properly.
2. You need the equipment for spraying--either a spray gun or airbrush and an air compressor.

The Spray Method

This is a great technique to use on both clay and bisque to create colors, textures, and slips. You can also apply transparent and colored glazes. It is a technique, however, that requires some practice and a little experimentation to master. You might want to start with some sample vessels to get the techniques down. As with any method, the type of clay and kiln affect the final outcome, but, with spraying, you will need to apply multiple coats and have patience as each coat dries. Even so, this is a technique that gives you plenty of room for creativity.

Let's look at the best method to make sure spraying on your glaze is successful. As with any technique, you want to ensure you're following the proper safety precautions. For this technique, you need the proper personal safety equipment as well as the spray booth. You'll need the respirator, goggles, and gloves, as well as good ventilation in your spray booth.

Clay/Glaze Compatibility

This really applies to any of the techniques we've talked about. It's important that your glaze and clay are compatible to get the best results. When you're selecting a glaze, you want it to match your type of clay so that you don't get bubbling, cracking, or crazing. You can test the compatibility if you're unsure. Just apply a small amount of glaze to a small piece of pottery before doing other pieces. Fire that piece in the temperature range of the clay material you're using and check your results. You don't want to take chances - the wrong glaze can be a costly mistake.

If you're working with different types of clays and glaze, keep notes on the results of your experiments. Particularly if you're making your own glaze, you'll want to note the recipes you've used and what works best. You might think you'll remember the recipe, but you almost certainly won't, and you'll regret not writing it down.

No Oils

As you're working with your glaze, you should ensure that you keep oils away from it, and that includes the oils on your hands. That's why you'll be wearing gloves and washing your hands when handling your pottery and the glaze materials. You also shouldn't use any lotions on your hands since those contain oils.

Prepare Your Pieces

After you've bisque fired your pottery at cone 04 so that it is sufficiently porous for the glaze to adhere well, you can sand it smooth. Wetting the piece and the sandpaper will make that an easier process and keep dust from blowing around. Once this is done, clean the piece well with a wet sponge to remove any remaining dust. This will help your glaze bind to the pottery.

Protect the Bottom

Once you've done this, you'll want to wax the bottom of the ceramic. This is a great tip for preventing glaze from dripping and sticking to the bottom. It's done by applying a small amount of wax resist to the bottom of the piece. That will allow you to use various kinds of glazes. If some does run down to the bottom, you can simply wipe it off with a damp sponge since the composition of the wax resist keeps it from sticking.

Prepare the Glaze

For spraying on glaze, you need to prepare a finely blended glaze product so that your spray gun won't get clogged. Begin by mixing your glaze thoroughly and then pour it through a sieve. Then, remix it so that you have an even consistency. Do this before you spray each piece. A good tip is to use an electric drill with a mixer attachment to make the task easier and to get a more thorough mix for your glaze.

Prepare Your Spray Gun and Spray Area

Now you'll want to have your spray gun at the ready. For that, you'll need your air compressor set up with your nozzle selections ready. You'll also want to prepare your spray booth by covering it with paper so that will save time cleaning up after you're done. You'll also want to ensure you have what you need in the booth. For example, you'll want a hand wheel in there for this process.

To prepare your spray gun, you'll need to test it to ensure it is spraying the proper amount of glaze. You'll also want to note the area it is covering as you spray. You'll want to ensure that the layers are not too thick or thin since either can result in streaking. Lastly, you should check your technique to make sure you can hold the gun steady and apply an even coat. That's also important for preventing streaks. One tip for this is to change the direction of spray when you're applying different layers.

Set It Up

Set the pottery on your hand wheel because you'll be rotating the piece as you're spraying. When you've got everything ready, it's time to go.

Coat the Inside First

As with the pouring method, coat the inside first. Be sure to hold the sprayer at a good distance to ensure an even texture for the glaze layer. Rotate the hand wheel as you coat the inside of the piece evenly and thoroughly. Clean your nozzle after every two to three layers that you apply of the same-colored glaze. You'll need to clean it even more frequently - after every layer - if you're using different colors. This will create a cleaner, finer glaze and help prevent your nozzle from becoming clogged. Use some warm water to clear the nozzle and then open the spray gun to clean it out.

You'll also want to let each layer dry thoroughly before applying another. That makes this a slower process if you have a lot of coats, but the result is worth the wait. Also, if you spray glaze on an area that has already been covered or you get some thick spots caused by runny glaze, you'll be tempted to wipe those up, but wait for it to dry thoroughly before removing them. You can use sandpaper to remove the excess when it's dry. If you try to wipe at wet glaze, you'll end up with a smudge or unwanted marks at that spot.

You should also check the thickness of your layers as you apply the glaze. Don't let them be too thick or too thin. For spray glaze, it should be the thickness of a regular T-shirt. Carefully use your fingernail to feel the thickness. If it's not right, you can make adjustments. All of this can be done as you're applying layers to the inside of the vessel. That way, you'll have everything just right when it comes time to do the outside. When you've finished the inside of the vessel, it's time to move on to the outside. You use the same techniques, but you'll have your spraying technique and glaze consistency just right.

Extra Tips for Glazing

These are a few extra tips that will make glazing much easier.

- **Kiln Wash or Cookie:** Kiln wash or cookies help to protect your kiln shelf and pottery by resisting glaze and other substances that you apply. Simply brush the kiln wash onto the kiln shelf, and it will help prevent pottery from sticking to it. A bisque cookie serves the same purpose.

- **Use a Rotary Tool**: A very thick layer of glaze can be difficult to remove, particularly if you forgot to sand it down. But, a handheld rotary tool will solve that. With it, you can simply grind melted (fired) glaze off your pottery, and you can also use it to sand the remaining parts of the pot.

- **Don't Use Multiple Glazes**: You might be tempted to think that using more than one glaze at the same time will save you time. The reality is that it results in more errors. Glazes begin to separate quickly after they have been applied, and the more glazes you use, the longer they have to sit and separate. Moreover, the final result of the glaze will only be seen after the vessel has been fired, so it's easy for them to mix, and, if that's not what you wanted, you'll be stuck with the result. Stick to a single glaze at a time, and you'll be able to keep everything organized and create great pieces.

- **Dry the Glaze Properly**: Glazing pottery takes a lot of patience. You have to let your glazed pieces dry adequately, and that really does take time. If you touch the glaze and it still feels cold to the touch, it's not dry. You should wait until it's room temperature to the touch before you put it in the kiln. Glazes do dry faster than greenware, but it's a good rule of thumb to allow your glazed pieces to dry overnight to be sure they are completely dried. You can simply load your kiln the next morning.

In conclusion, spray glazing is an excellent technique for glazing and underglazing. You get even coats that nicely float across your pottery. It takes some patience and the right equipment, but it's a great way to create an amazing piece of art. You'll definitely be pleased with the results using this technique.

Chapter Summary

In this chapter, we've discussed the technique of spraying on glaze. Specifically, we've covered the following topics:

- The advantages and disadvantages of spray glazing;

- The importance of preparing your tools, spray area, and using personal safety equipment;

- The steps to ensure you're using the right glaze that's compatible with your clay;

- The specific step-by-step instructions for spray glazing;

- Some extra tips for this technique.

In the next chapter, you will learn about a few other techniques that can be used for applying glaze to your ceramic pieces.

Chapter Nine: Other Glaze Application Techniques

There are a number of other techniques that can be used to apply glaze. The ones described in the previous chapters are the most common, and they're good ones for beginners to start with. There are, however, other ways to achieve many different finishes. Let's take a look at some of the more standard ones.

Trailing Method

This is also called the slip trail because it makes use of a glaze slip. In fact, there are all sorts of pottery decorating techniques that will use a slip glaze in the process. That's because it allows you to create a range of effects, from very linear designs to highly textual ones and from very fluid to very hard-edged designs. Slip trailing is a more widely-known method for this type of decorating with a slip. It basically delivers a stream of slip to either damp or leather-hard clay using some kind of dispenser.

It's a great way to create a design of fluid, gestural marks that will either settle on top or sink into your primary glaze. Before doing that, you should always test for the compatibility of the glazes in a similar way to that described previously for testing the compatibility of your clay with your glaze. Simply apply your glazes to a small piece of pottery in the same way you intend to on your primary piece and fire it to see if the glazes can be used together.

Advantages of Trail Glazing

1. It allows you to create patterns or motifs on your ceramics.
2. Compared with other approaches, not too much glaze is required for this technique.

Disadvantages of Trail Glazing

1. It's more time-consuming, and you can't use it if you're working on a large quantity of ceramics.
2. You will need to understand your colors thoroughly. Either that, or you shouldn't use too many colors.

Double-Dipping Method

Double-dipping is also called secondary glazing. The technique is to apply glazes where the ceramics have already been dipped in a container of glaze. You do this after the ceramic has been sitting for a few minutes. You also dip it again later into the same or another container of glaze. To dip the glaze a second or third time, you use the same techniques as described in the chapter on dipping.

The consistency of the glazes used for this technique should be like a heavy cream. You dip the ceramic in the glaze and leave it for three seconds. That's about it, but let's look at the advantages and disadvantages of this method.

Advantages of Double-Dipping

1. Like the regular dipping method, it's easy and fast.
2. It's also easier to correct for errors.

Disadvantages of Double-Dipping

1. It requires a large amount of glaze, which makes it untenable if you want to do a lot of ceramics.
2. The glazes used are more fluid than those for the brushing technique, making them that much more susceptible to running.

The Stencilling Method

If you're decorating your ceramics using the brushing method, this can sometimes cause your work to look unprofessional. An alternative to using paint brushes to decorate your pottery is to use vellum stencils to create precise designs using glaze. With this method, your finished pieces will have a more elegant appearance and will seem more refined than if you just use paint brushes to paint on your designs.

To use the stencilling method, follow these steps:

1. Put your vessel on a flat surface like your work table countertop. The ceramic should have been bisque fired at this point.
2. Put a vellum stencil on the vessel where you want the design and tape it down with art tape. This type of tape can be used

and removed without leaving any residue or marks behind. The vellum stencil is good because it's flexible and can be wrapped around contoured surfaces.

3. Using a sponge brush, apply the glaze onto the vessel by dabbing over the stencil. Just apply glaze to the uncovered area of the stencil. Be careful around the edges of the stencil as glaze could spill onto areas you don't want decorated.

4. After you've finished applying the glaze, remove the art tape and the stencil. Allow the glaze to completely dry. This can take several hours and you want to make sure it is thoroughly dried.

5. Fire the clay at a high heat for six hours to get a glass-like decoration in the shape of the stenciled pattern.

Marbling Method

Marbling is something you can do at any time in the process of pottery creation, and that includes the glaze application. When you're marbling as you apply glaze, follow these steps:

1. Use a natural or synthetic, fine-textured pottery sponge to apply the glaze.

2. For secondary glaze application with a contrasting glaze, be sure to use a very porous sponge that will create interesting patterns.

3. You'll need to work quickly for the best results, so be sure to keep your tools to hand, including a dump bucket for contaminated glazes.

4. Choose three or four glazes that you would like to marbleize. Pour the quantities you need into measuring cups and place them within reach.

5. Quickly pour each color into your pot and swirl the glazes around to get a marbled appearance. Don't mix them too much.

6. Dump all of the glazes quickly out of the pot and into the dump bucket.

7. Apply the marbled glaze to the inside of the pot and allow it to dry completely.

8. Pour on glaze to the exterior of the pot--you'll want to experiment with the technique so that you can control the flow of the glazes better. You can also run your fingers through the glaze to make it thicker in some areas and thinner in others--just like finger painting.

These glaze techniques give you some other options for decorating your ceramics. Play around with each approach until you feel comfortable, and then you can try other methods. Don't be afraid to experiment and let your creativity flow just as much as the glazes flow!

Chapter Summary

In this chapter, we've covered several other techniques for applying glaze to ceramic vessels. Specifically, we've covered the following concepts:

- The trailing method;

- The double-dipping method;

- The stencilling method;

- The marbling method.

In the next chapter, you will learn about firing clay.

Chapter Ten: Stages of Clay

It's important to understand the stages of clay so that you can better understand the application of glazes and slips and how that interacts with clay. Pottery goes through seven stages to arrive at the finished product. Let's take a look at each of these stages.

Dry Clay Stage: This is the initial point in which you find clay. Dry clay is composed of fine particles that were formed from volcanic ash millions of years ago. The most common type that is used in pottery is called Ball Clay. Ball Clays contain quartz, mica, kaolinite, iron, titanium, and some other minerals.

Taking the water out of clay makes it lighter and easier to store and ship. In fact, you can store dry clay as long as you need to--it won't ever stink or turn rotten. Wet clay, on the other hand, can be invaded by certain contaminants that will make it go bad. Dry clay also gives you more options for modification with the addition of things like grog, colorants, or fine sand before you add water back into it.

You can buy dry clay in a powder form and then just add water to work it. You can choose from different colors, textures, and cone sizes. You can also use recycled clay and rehydrate it for new use. If you break up recycled clay into small pieces with a hammer, when you rehydrate it, the moisture will get back into it faster and more evenly. You can probably also get out some of your frustrations that way!

Finally, it is possible to go dig up some clay depending on where you live. You can even find different colors and textures of clay. Many potters feel like this helps them feel more connected to the earth.

Slip Stage: The slip stage happens when you add water to the clay. How much and how runny the slip is depends on what you want to do with it. There are a couple of different uses:

a) **Glue**--Slip acts like a glue that holds the clay together as you add certain features like handles or decorative pieces. The way you use it to attach something like a handle is to criss-cross lines where you want to attach the feature and then apply slip there. For this purpose, you want the slip to be the same consistency as mixed sour cream. You don't want it to be too stiff or too runny.

b) **Decoration**--You can use applicator bottles with different-sized tips to make some beautiful designs with slip. You can even add powdered colors such as mason stain. It comes in pink, blue, and green, as well as other colors. If you're using a slip for decorating, it should be the consistency of well-mixed sour cream.

c) Mold slips--If you're using a slip for a mold, you want it to be runny and have the consistency of heavy cream since you'll be pouring the clay into the mold. That's why it shouldn't be as thick as something like a decorative slip.

When you're working with slips, it's helpful to have a bucket of slip set to one side. That way, you don't have to stop what you're doing to make more. You can keep it from drying out by adding water to get it back to the consistency you want. It also helps to add a bit of vinegar occasionally to keep your slip fresh. When you're applying a slip for decoration, it's best to use cone 10 stoneware. That allows you to fire the clay at a higher temperature, and you can also add colorants as you want. Finally, remember to watch the consistency of your flip if you're using it for decorating. You don't want it to be either too runny or too thick.

Plastic Stage of Clay: This is the fun stage where the clay is workable. It's malleable (flexible), and this is where you create your vessel. You can shape it into anything you want. You are only limited by your creativity. Once you have your basic vessel, the clay will begin to lose its flexibility, but you can then commence with decorations. You can trim it, attach something, or decorate it. The only thing you can't do with it is mold it anymore.

Leather Hard Stage: This is the stage where the clay has hardened even more. During this stage, you can trim it, add handles, and make any other alterations you need to make before it gets too hard. It feels like soft leather at this stage, and, obviously, that's where the name comes from. At this point, you can handle it without leaving finger marks on it.

There are also different stages of leather hardness, and you want to wait until it is just right before working with it. If it is too soft, you won't be able to trim it properly and attachments like handles won't stay there. If it gets too dry, it will be too hard to work with. If it's too soft, you can simply wait for it to dry a little bit more, but if it gets too hard, there won't be much you can do. If you wrap the clay in plastic, it will slow down the drying time. That helps if you don't have the time at the moment to finish the piece. In fact, sealing it in plastic can give you up to a week to trim it.

It's at this stage that you can also apply an underglaze. You can apply patterns or even transfer pictures when it is in this stage.

Bone Dry Stage: This is the stage of clay when the moisture is completely out of the clay. At this stage, it is dry enough to bisque fire. That process can take a week or longer, depending on where you live. It will take longer if you live in a humid climate. You do want the clay to be bone dry, so if you don't think it's dry enough, wait a little longer until you're sure. You can even do what is called candling your clay to dry it out. That's where you put it in your kiln on a super low heat to remove any last moisture.

In this stage, you can also apply an underglaze. You should apply two to three coats. Make sure each coat is completely dry before applying the next one. When you go to place your bone dry clay in the kiln, the pieces can touch unless they have an underglaze. You don't want that underglaze to touch other pottery or it will transfer the color to that piece. That's why you can also apply the underglaze after the bisque firing.

Bisque ware Stage: This is the stage where the clay is fired between Cone 08 (1,728 degrees Fahrenheit, 942 degrees Celsius) and Cone -4 (1,945 degrees Fahrenheit, 1063 degrees Celsius). This is done to remove the chemically bonded water and impurities in the clay. This firing also changes the clay permanently by making it harder, but still porous, so that it can absorb glazes better.

Once you have fired your bisqueware, you then proceed to prepare it for glazing by cleaning it with a damp sponge so you can remove any dirt, dust, or fingerprints. Then, you'll dry the piece thoroughly before applying underglaze or glaze.

Glaze Firing Stage: This is the stage where you're finishing your ceramic piece. The glazes you applied will melt to the pottery and become glassy in appearance. Your colorful patterns and designs will come to life at this point. Since you don't know exactly what your glazes will look like until they've been fired, it's particularly exciting waiting for the pieces to come out of the kiln. As we discussed previously, there are three firing settings you can use:

a) **Low-fire**--usually cone 04 with an average temperature around 1,800 degrees Fahrenheit (982 degrees Celsius). If you place a low-fire clay in higher temperatures, the pottery can melt into the kiln shelf. That's why it's important to know the cone size of the clay you're working with and to make sure it matches with any glazes you're using.

b) **Mid-fire**--usually cone 5 or 6 at approximately 2,250 degrees Fahrenheit (1,232 degrees Celsius). When you're looking at the cone size of your clay, be aware if the number has a 0 before it. This is a different firing temperature than if it doesn't. 05 is not the same as 5.

c) **High-fire**--This is typically cone 10 with a temperature of approximately 2,380 degrees Fahrenheit (1,304 degrees Celsius). If your clay is not rated to cone 10, it will melt in the kiln, and it will not vitrify. That means it won't be waterproof. Remember, your glaze also has to match.

Once you've set the kiln to the proper temperature, you might also want to put a five or ten-minute hold on that temperature when it reaches its peak. Then you fire up the kiln and in about 12 to 20 hours, you'll be able to see the results of your hard work. The length of time depends on the size of your kiln as well as the rate of heat per hour and the time it takes to cool down. When it's all done, you can unload and admire your work.

Enjoy: The last stage is to enjoy the fruits of your labor. You can eat or drink out of it, admire your creative decorations, give it to someone you love, or sell it to someone who wants it. You've worked hard to produce this piece, and you deserve to take a moment to enjoy what you've created as well as pat yourself on the back for having taken part in an art style that has been around for thousands of years.

Kiln Tips for Beginners

We've gone through the different stages of clay, but you might also like a few kiln tips for newcomers. Using a kiln can be a little intimidating, and these tips will help you gain confidence. Here are ten things that can help as you get started;

1. It seems scary, but it's not that bad. After a while, you'll think of the kiln as just a large toaster oven!

2. There are different kilns for every kind of potter. You might be a part-time hobbyist who needs a small home kiln, or a working artist who needs a medium to large kiln. If you're that hobbyist, you don't have to spend a lot of money to get a huge kiln. You can get a great, sturdy, brand-new compact kiln for around the same cost as a Mac laptop. If you're a working artist and need a larger kiln, it will pay for itself and then some.

3. The electricity usage is not as costly as you think. A regular electric schedule on an electric kiln will cost you about $7.50 per fire. Some energy usage plans may allow you to have different prices for off-peak hours. If that's the case, you can even get it down to about $4 per fire. This is where you want to make a bunch of items and fire them all at once to keep your bills manageable.

4. Setup is pretty easy, and most companies offer help. If you're using an electric kiln, check with an electrician to make sure you have the appropriate outlets for your kiln location. Remember also to check that you have the appropriate amperage. If you have to have a new outlet and switch installed, it will cost approximately $100.

No matter what kind of kiln you're using, you should make sure you have a vent, and most companies sell those along with the kiln.

You'll also need that furniture to match the size of your kiln. For the kiln shelves, you'll need to 'wash' them before use. You get a special powdered mixture for that; add water, and apply it with a paintbrush in two even coats. That will keep the glaze drips from permanently sticking to your shelves. It's roughly comparable with baking spray.

After that, you want to test fire with the cone before you actually fire your work. This will set your kiln. After firing, the cone should be bent over to appear as though it is kissing the shelf. Be aware that when you start the kiln, it will make clicking noises as it revs up.

Don't leave the kiln unattended if it is on. Be sure someone is at home at all times while it is running. Also, remember that it will take six to eight hours for your kiln to cool, and you want to wait until it is at room temperature before opening the lids and removing items.

Be sure that you set glazed pieces on stilts or cookies so they don't stick to the shelves. You don't have to stilt unglazed bisque, however.

1. It is possible to fix mistakes. You can use a small knife or sandpaper, for example, to remove smeared underglaze, and you can use a rotary tool like a Dremel drill to remove unwanted glaze. You can then refire the piece.

2. You can make and fire small and big pieces together.

3. You can make your own molds out of silicone mold makers and some cornstarch. You could also make candy-making molds. This is handy for mass-production pieces.

4. You might think about hosting a private pottery studio where you can charge other people to fire their pottery.

This can help you offset the costs of firing your own pottery and buying the kiln.

5. Keep the kiln supplies in the same area. You want your standing rack for pieces that are drying to be close to the kiln, but don't put it in the way of the door where you're loading pieces. You also don't want to have to keep walking around the rack. It's easy to bump it and knock it over.

6. If the power goes out in the middle of a fire, just restart the kiln and let it run through again.

It's also a smart idea to maintain your kiln by using a vacuum to clean out debris and checking to see if your stilts need to be retired (they will get messed up with multiple firings and cause your pieces to topple over if you don't get new ones).

Chapter Summary

In this chapter, we've discussed the stages of clay and some tips for using a kiln. Specifically, we've talked about the following topics:

- The eight stages of clay--well, the last one is for you and not the clay!

- Tips to help newcomers feel more comfortable using a kiln;

- Tips for maintaining your kiln.

In the next chapter, you will learn about several different glaze recipes.

Chapter Eleven: Ceramic Glaze Recipes

When you're first starting out, you might want to begin with prepared glaze recipes until you get comfortable with the procedure, but you're likely to progress to the point where you'll want to mix your own glaze recipes. That will really allow you to expand your creativity. Let's look a little more closely at all the reasons you might want to make your own glazes.

Benefits of Making Your Own Glazes

First of all, while there are many beautiful ready-made glazes on the market, the truth is that your creativity becomes rather limited if you're only purchasing prepared glazes. You can get them in powder form, and all you have to do is add water to mix them. That does give you some experience with mixing, sieving, and, of course, applying the glaze. Additionally, they are typically much more forgiving if you apply them too thickly or too thinly, or if they are not fired at the exact right temperature. While that is a perfectly acceptable way to go if you're not comfortable making your own glazes, there are some benefits quite apart from the creativity that you might want to bear in mind.

First, you will have complete control over your glaze. You can decide how glossy or matte you want it to be. You can have a greater variety of colors or vary the amounts of other effects like speckles. You can choose all of the glaze variables, including things like the melting temperature. To change any variable, you simply adjust the recipe. That allows you the room to experiment and create unique glazes.

Another very significant benefit to making your own glazes is the cost factor. It is quite simply less expensive to make your own glaze. In fact, it's approximately fifty percent less expensive, and that saving really adds up with each kiln load. If you're going to go down that route, however, it will be advantageous to understand a little more about the chemistry of making glazes. So, we shall start with the main components.

Main Components of Glaze

There are three main components of a glaze:

1. **The glass formers**: These are mostly composed of silica, and they are the part of the glaze that actually creates the glass. While there are some technicalities to these, we're basically just talking about sand. If you were to try to make a glaze with

just silica, you would need a very high-firing temperature to do so. To avoid that, you will use a flux.

2. **Fluxes**: These are the additives that help the glaze melt at a lower temperature. Those glazes that are considered low-temperature glazes have much more flux added than high-temperature glazes.

3. **Stabilizers**: These are two substances--alumina and boron--that keep the glaze attached to the pot. Without stabilizers, the glaze would simply run off of the pot and onto the kiln shelf when it melted. Stabilizers stiffen the glaze so that it sticks to the pot.

Developing a Recipe

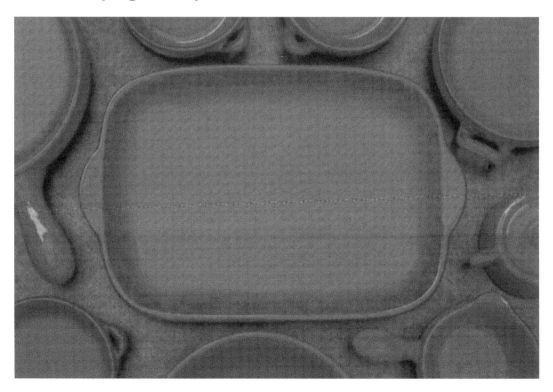

Now that you know the main components, you can move on to actually developing your recipes. This chapter will present some recipes you can use at first before moving on to your own mixes, but when you do start mixing your own, you want to have a good understanding of what additives you want to use for things like making your glaze safe for food or creating the appearance you want.

To create your own glaze from scratch, you will need to decide on the following factors before you create a recipe:

- The cone temperature you will use to fire the glaze. This is also determined by the clay you will use as well as the maximum temperature of your kiln;

- Whether you will be firing in an oxidation or reduction atmosphere;

- Do you want to have a matte or glossy surface;

- What color or colors do you want to create;

- Does the glaze need to be food-safe?

As you create your recipe, you might start with what are called limit formulas. These are formulas designed to help you create reliable, stable, predictable, and functional glazes that will allow for the use of multiple colors and that won't blister, crawl, pinhole, or leach. In other words, if you stay within the guidelines of the limit formula, you'll get a glaze that will work well and give you a solid foundation for understanding how to create glazes. Basically, limit formulas are guidelines for creating good glazes.

Limit formulas are not, however, simply an average recipe; rather, they are conservative guidelines for producing well-melted and durable glazes. They are the result of experimentation by professional technicians who have tried different recipes to determine the proper balances for oxide amounts. Oxides are the additives you put in a glaze, and some contradict one another. For example, oxides that encourage hardness don't promote stability. So, you don't want to add too much of that kind of oxide without balancing it out with proper stabilizers.

The term limit formula has created some controversy since potters are an independent group and don't like to feel like they are being restricted. This really isn't designed to limit you, however, but it is designed to give you suggestions based on experiments showing what works and what doesn't. Some have even suggested it would be better to use the term 'suggestion formulas' instead of limit formulas.

While you can certainly experiment as you would like with different formulas, the limit formulas are designed to help you understand the oxide levels in your glaze that will produce a solid result. You should definitely stick to the limit formulas if your glaze is going to be applied to a food surface. Some potters will take great pains to ensure all of their glazes are within the food-safe limit formulas since someone might decide to drink out of a non-traditional ceramic. While the limit formulas don't guarantee safety, they are a good place to start.

Limit formulas also give you a good idea of how much flux to add for each cone range, and how to make adjustments to the silica and alumina ratios for the amount of gloss you want to produce. Coloring oxides are more difficult to adjust since they are more dependent on the atmosphere of your kiln. Nonetheless, by taking good notes and keeping track of your results, you can create effective recipes for producing the colors you're trying to achieve.

Calculating Glaze Recipes

While you can go about calculating your glazes recipes the hard way through trial and error with a pen and paper, there are some websites that can help make that job a lot easier. The following websites allow you to simply enter your glaze ingredients and the percentage for each one--adding up to 100 percent--and they will simulate the glaze results. Here are a few you might want to try:

- Glaze simulator

- Insight live

- Glazy.org

These are great resources, and you can even store your recipes in their databases. You can also browse other people's recipes and there are forums to discuss your work. They can really help you as you get started making your own glaze recipes.

Buying Glaze Ingredients

The nice thing about the main ingredients for glaze is that they are fairly inexpensive. The most expensive base ingredients are the frits or, basically, ground glass. They are about five times more expensive than something like clay or quartz. The good thing is that they are used in smaller quantities. Therefore, you don't have to buy as much to make your glaze.

Additionally, some of the coloring oxides can be costly, but you can usually also buy those in small quantities. For example, for glazes that use cobalt, they will contain only about 1 percent of that oxide, so you don't need much of it. Typically, you want to figure out your recipe and calculate how much you need of each ingredient to make a five-kilogram batch. That will be enough to fill your glaze bucket. By calculating the ingredients you need for each batch, you can avoid spending too much on ingredients that are just going to sit around on your shelf for months.

Equipment for Making Glazes

Another great thing about making your own glaze is that you don't need much equipment. You'll need some five to ten liter round buckets with lids--this is the minimum size you'll want to get for dipping--a sieve of #80 size mesh or finer (which you can find at ceramic suppliers), a typical kitchen whisk, your respirator for safety--with a p100 rated filter, a digital scale, and a large paint brush, just like you would use for painting your walls. That's it: you're ready to make glaze.

Mixing Your First Recipe

Okay, with your ingredients and equipment ready, you're ready to mix your first recipe. You want your glaze recipe to add up to approximately 100 percent--some recipes add up to just 98 percent, but that's okay as long as it's pretty close to 100 percent. Now, you need to decide how much to make. It's a good idea to make around 100 grams of ingredients with the same amount of water to test on a small ceramic piece. That way, you can make sure your glaze will work well. After you've done that, you can make the glaze you need for your piece. To give you an idea of how much you'll need, if you're dipping a mug, you'll need around 2 kilograms of dry ingredients to mix with approximately 2 liters of water.

Your recipes will indicate the percentage of each ingredient. Let's take a look at a mid-fire recipe to give you an idea of how to calculate the amount of dry ingredients you need for a 2 kilogram batch of glaze. Here's the recipe:

Mid-Fire Glaze Recipe #1

- 20.00 Wollastonite

- 10.00 Calcium Borate Frit

- 20.00 China Clay

- 15.00 Quartz

- 35.00 Soda Feldspar

The numbers indicate the percentage of each ingredient, so 20 percent Wollastonite, 10 percent Calcium Borate Frit, and so on. You'll notice that everything adds up to 100 percent. Now, to calculate how much you need of the dry ingredients to get those percentages in a 2 kilogram batch, you simply multiply the percentage by 20 to get the following amounts:

- 400g Wollastonite

- 200g Calcium Borate Frit

- 400g China Clay

- 300g Quartz

- 700g Soda Feldspar

You'll notice that these ingredients add up to 2000 grams which is 2 kilograms. If you needed a 5 kilogram batch for your glaze, you would multiply the percentages by 50 instead of 20. That would be enough to dip a larger piece like a bowl or vase. Once you've calculated the weights needed for the dry ingredients, it's time to get them mixed. Just follow these instructions:

1. Put on your safety equipment, including your respirator;

2. Fill your bucket with the starting amount of water--in our example here, 2 liters;

3. Set a container for your dry ingredients on your scale and zero it out;

4. Add your first ingredient until it's at the appropriate weight, and then carefully pour the weighted ingredient into the bucket of water;

5. Repeat that process for each ingredient. Be sure to keep good notes and cross each ingredient off the list after you've added it to the bucket;

6. When all ingredients are added, add more water if you need to--the glaze should be a consistency that is between milk and single cream thickness;

7. Put your sieve on top of another clean bucket;

8. Pour the glaze mixture into the sieve in stages while using a paintbrush to mix the glaze within the sieve. Use the bristles of the brush to help move the glaze through the sieve;

9. Once mixed, clean the area and your tools before removing your respirator;

10. Let the glaze sit for 24 hours before you use it so that all particles will be properly soaked into the water. Then, mix it with your whisk before and during the application of the glaze onto your piece.

More Glaze Recipes

Now that you know the procedure for mixing the glaze, here are some glaze recipes you can use to get started. The above recipe was a mid-fire, cone 6 glaze recipe. So, let's begin with another mid-fire glaze recipe, and then we'll move on to low and high-fire recipes.

Mid-Fire Recipe #2

This is for a matte glaze base that is fired at cone 6. It fires to create a hard utilitarian surface with good working properties, and you can blend in the glossy if you don't want it to be too matte in its finish.

- 17.40 Ferro Frit 3124

- 23.50 Dolomite

- 26.90 Silica

- 18.30 EP Kaolin

- 13.90 Calcined Kaolin

These add up to 100 percent. This recipe creates the best suspension if you make it thixotropic by adding Epsom salts with a target-specific gravity of 1.43 to 1.44. That's achieved by adding approximately 90 percent water to 100 percent of the dry ingredients. For example, if you've got 1000 grams of powder, you'll want to add 900 grams of water. Then, add 1 gram of Epsom salts to increase the thixotropy. The result should be creamy, and it should gel after just a few seconds of standing still.

It's also very important to note that the degree of matteness depends on the cooling rate of the firing. So, if you have a free-fall in a lightly-loaded or smaller kiln, your pieces will cool fast, and that will produce a silky matte surface. If you have a heavily loaded kiln, the cooling will be slower, and that will produce a matter, drier surface. You can do test firings to determine your cooling rate, and you can also add in some glossy glaze if you'd like the results to have more shine. You also should know that some colors will cause this recipe to matte more than others, so you might need to make adjustments depending on the colors you're using.

Low-Fire Glaze Recipes

These recipes are for glazes that will be fired below cone 04. Two are presented to get you started.

Low-Fire Glaze Recipe #1

This is a cone 03, white engobe recipe that produces a stoneware or white slip that matches red Zero3 stoneware.

- 10.00 Nepheline Syenite

- 42.00 Tile #6 Kaolin

- 25.00 Ferro Frit 3110

- 20.00 Silica

- 5.00 National Standard Bentonitc

This adds up to 102 percent, but, as was mentioned previously, that's close enough. This recipe produces a slip--engobe--and a body recipe. It creates a low-fire stoneware body, slip, and glaze that is dubbed Zero3. You should note that the frit used in this recipe amplifies the colors, and you can apply colored slips during the leather-hard stage of clay. Then, you can finish it with a clear glaze that you can dip after bisque firing. Let the slurry gel when using it as a slip so it will hang onto the piece.

Low-Fire Glaze Recipe #2

This is for cone 03 terra cotta stoneware.

- 45.00 Plainsman 3D

- 50.00 Redart

- 5.00 National Standard Bentonite

- 10.00 Ferro Frit 3110

- 1.00 Yellow Iron Oxide

- 0.25 Barium Carbonate

This adds up to 111.25, but that's also fine. This is a good glaze for applying to the body, and if you're careful to make sure there are no imperfections in the glaze surface, you can fire this at cone 04, and it will produce a strong ceramic.

High-Fire Glaze Recipes

These are high-fire glaze recipes designed for firing at a minimum of cone 10.

High-Fire Glaze Recipe #1

This recipe creates a matte finish with a silky surface.

- 5.50 Wollastonite

- 28.50 Custer Feldspar

- 28.00 EPK

- 15.00 Silica

- 19.00 Dolomite

- 4.00 Gerstley Borate

This totals 100. This recipe is one that has been effectively used for many years. You can add colorants and opacifiers if you want to add some beautiful classic earthy reduction effects. One that is really popular is to add 3.5 Rutile and 10 Zircopax for a bamboo effect on the finished piece. Additionally, many matte glazes that are made with dolomite or talc don't have a good balance, and you end up with crazing, staining, or other problems. This particular glaze recipe, however, has a great silky surface with none of those problems.

High-Fire Glaze Recipe #2

This is a cone 10 glossy transparent base glaze that is used for porcelains and whitewares.

- 27.00 Custer Feldspar

- 20.50 EPK

- 26.50 Silica

- 23.50 Wollastonite

- 2.50 Zinc Oxide

This totals 100. This glaze has been used by numerous potters all around the world. It was originally designed as a porcelain insulator glaze, and it's a good one to use as a base for a large range of colors and effects. The ingredient percentages used in this recipe help prevent crazing and cracking while drying.

These recipes are presented as a starting point for you to learn how to create your own recipes. There are different ways you can vary these recipes to create your own unique glaze. In some cases, substitutions will give you a different color or effect. When you're experimenting with making your own recipes, you want to document everything, and that includes your ingredients, methods of mixing, and the effects you obtained. If something went wrong, make a note of that as well. Then, it's always nice if you can share your recipes with other potters, like yourself, who are looking to mix their own glazes. You can share your recipes in many of the same online forums listed above. You'll be helping other potters learn, and you'll be expanding the database of glaze recipes.

Chapter Summary

In this chapter, we've discussed glaze recipes and how to make your own glaze. Specifically, we've discussed the following topics:

- The benefits of making your own glaze;

- The main components of glaze;

- How to develop a glaze recipe;

- How to simulate your recipe;

- The equipment you'll need to make your own glaze;

- How to mix your ingredients;

- Two high, mid, and low-fire recipes for glazes.

In the next chapter, you will learn about developing a business out of your pottery hobby.

Chapter Twelve: Going Pro with Your Talent

If you really love making pottery, you've likely thought about starting your own ceramic business. Of course, there are many things you need to consider before doing something like that, but the first thing you want to do is create a good business plan. In that plan, you might think about the many ways you can make money in this business.

Where to Sell Your Wares

Of course, you'll likely want to sell your ceramics, and there are certainly many online and brick and mortar businesses where you can do that. You can sell your work, for example, on an art site like

Etsy, you can create your own website, or you could work through something like eBay or Amazon.com. There are certainly many virtual outlets, but your biggest concern will be in the marketing of your products. It's a competitive industry. There are lots of artists selling their work online, and you'll have to find a way to stand out from the crowd.

You could also open a brick and mortar shop to sell your work, but that will require much more of an upfront investment than you might be willing to make. You'll also still need to attract your customers, and having a specialty niche is a good way to do that. Maybe you specialize in outdoor ceramics like garden gnomes, or perhaps ceramic dinnerware is more your style. Whatever suits you best, you'll want to direct your efforts towards being the best in that niche.

Another option is to sell your work on consignment through other shops that may or may not sell similar products. To do this, you would have to make a deal with the shop owners, and they will take a commission for every piece that sells, or they might charge you a fee to display your work in their shop.

What About Teaching?

Another way you can make this into a business is to offer pottery classes. To do this, you'll need a large enough space to work with students, and for them to have enough room to make their creations. This can be a fun way to do it since the students can often come up with new ideas, and a learning environment is highly creative by its nature. You might also work through a local university or college to teach a pottery class. They have varying requirements with regard to the educational level their instructors possess, so this may or may not work for you, but there are usually many art studios or free learning institutions that don't have the same requirements.

Be a Part of the Community

Whichever way you decide to develop a business out of your hobby, it's a great idea to really become a part of the artisan community where you live. Go to art shows and display your work, host a pottery-making workshop, or rent out your kiln to other potters. You might even decide to collaborate with other artisans and open a kind of cooperative studio where everyone can share expenses and profits. Remember that every time you have the opportunity to display your work, you're getting your name and talent out there.

Other Expert Tips

1. Take it a step at a time. Don't rush into opening a business. Give yourself some time and experience by making various pieces, and then that also builds up your inventory. Also, keep careful records, and if you find that something isn't working--a particular color is not selling or a specific kind of vessel doesn't move--then be open to changing it up. If you want to make your business successful, you have to produce the kinds of things that people will buy.

2. Create an internship and use interns to help. Interns make great assistants, and when one leaves, there's usually another one waiting for the opportunity to work with you. Check with your local college to see if they have any intern programs. You might even liaise with them to start one.

3. Be prepared to clean. Many first-time business owners aren't prepared for the amount of cleaning they'll be doing. With a pottery workshop, there will be a lot to clean up on a regular basis, so make sure you have an extra mop bucket and a powerful vacuum cleaner.

4. Get a pugmill or clay mixer. This will be a game-changer for you. When you're doing this professionally, you'll want to be as efficient as possible. These devices will help you mix your clay, and they can help you recycle clay as well. If you're working in a cooperative-type business, you can even provide your members with recycled clay.

5. Use social media to the fullest to market your wares. When you're running a business, it's all about marketing. You want to get as many people as possible to see what

you're making and have the opportunity to buy them. Social media offers a far-reaching platform where you can put out posts about your latest projects, disperse your best glaze recipes, announce pottery competitions for people to participate in, and direct people to your business website. Most of this can be done for free, so use this tool to build your brand.

6. Ask for help. Don't feel as though asking for help means you've failed in some way. Ask for help when you need it. The potter community is usually a pretty open, sharing community, and most people will offer you advice if you go to them. You might also ask family, friends, and colleagues for help and suggestions. You may well find that they're rooting for your success almost as much as you are.

Opening your own business in any discipline is always complicated, but, if you work at becoming the best potter you can and being a part of your local artisan community, it is possible to turn your beloved hobby into your business. Be prepared to put in the hours and promote yourself, and you'll find there are many ways to have a successful ceramic business.

Chapter Summary

In this chapter, we've discussed how to turn your ceramic hobby into a business. Specifically, we've discussed the following topics:

- Where to sell your wares;

- The possibility of teaching about pottery making;

- The importance of becoming part of the artisan community;

- Other tips that can help you succeed.

The next chapter will present a few final thoughts.

Final Words

Learning how to mix and apply ceramic glazes is a rich and rewarding part of the pottery-making process. It gives you much more flexibility and allows you to be infinitely more creative. It's an important part of making ceramics, and, in this book, you've learned the many factors you need to consider to apply glazes correctly.

As a ceramicist, you're part of history. Perhaps you've never thought about it in that sense, but it's perfectly true. It's a long history of artisans going back thousands of years to when our ancestors started making ceramic vessels. They are objects that have actually been quite essential for humans. With ceramic vessels, it became possible to store surplus food items and carry things it would otherwise be difficult to transport.

The application of glazes was a giant step forward in the history of pottery-making since it allowed craftsmen to make waterproof vessels. What you've learned in this book has real-world, important applications. Now you're part of that venerated history of artisans contributing to the craft.

You've learned about the chemistry of mixing and applying glazes to your ceramic vessels, the equipment you'll need to do that, and the types of glazes you can use for your work. You've also learned the different ways to apply glaze, including dipping, spraying, painting, pouring, and many others. This gives you the knowledge to experiment with the ways you like best.

Moreover, you've learned about the stages of clay and how the clay interacts with the glaze to form a hardened surface that makes the vessel durable. You've also learned about how to use glazes to create unique and colorful decorations. With the glaze recipes presented in this book, you have a starting point for mixing your own glazes and creating your own recipes.

Finally, you've learned about the considerations for opening your own pottery business. You can take your pottery art to a whole new level, one that allows you to turn your hobby into a business you'll love. You're now part of a community of artists who are constantly striving to create better and more beautiful pieces.

There's nothing like allowing yourself to get lost in creating a piece of art. It's a goal like no other that allows you to express your artistic vision for your work. It lets you share something you uniquely created with the world, and there's little else in this world that is nearly as satisfying as that. When your friends, family, colleagues, and clients are amazed by something you created, you're bound to experience a sense of pride and satisfaction.

To share your artistic vision with those you love and the community at large is a privilege that relatively few people are able to enjoy. By learning these techniques, you're improving your artistic abilities and giving yourself more creative opportunities to express yourself. You should be delighted that you're taking this opportunity to improve your skills, and you should waste no time in having fun with what you've learned.

Experiment with your ideas as you learn to mix and apply glazes in different ways. Soon, you'll find you're teaching others what you've learned. Learning to glaze your own work will allow you to take your ceramic skills to a whole new level, perhaps even a professional one. So, congratulate yourself for learning some new techniques, go out and practice those techniques, and share your work with the world. It needs all the beauty it can get - now you have the means to contribute to that!

Made in United States
Troutdale, OR
08/19/2024